An Introduction to Bookkeeping

Suitable for the

AAT Accounting Qualification in

Processing Bookkeeping Transactions

Control Accounts, Journals

and the Banking System

and AAT Certificate in Bookkeeping

Revision Kit

(4th EDITION)

Alan Dawson, B.Ed (Hons), MAAT

Edited by Rose Crockett, BA (Hons)

PremierBooks

Published by:

Premier Books Ltd
Prince Henry Drive
Queens Road
Immingham
North East Lincolnshire
DN40 1QY
Telephone 01469 570290

Contents

The Author

Alan Dawson, Author

Alan Dawson

Certificate of Education

Bachelor of Education (Hons)

Member of the Association of Accounting Technicians

Qualified Teacher and Assessor

Alan is a qualified teacher. He gained his honours degree in education from Nottingham University and he went on to teach Mathematics, Modern Languages and Music in schools for 18 years.

He then turned his attention to accountancy, qualifying from the AAT and taking up various accounting roles both in private practice and industry. He spent 6 years in a large company in management accounts while at the same time taking private clients for help with bookkeeping, payroll, VAT and taxation.

From March 2006 he has been a tutor at Premier Training, with over 300 students worldwide under his guidance at one time or another.

About this Book

This Revision Kit is designed to be used alongside the An Introduction to Bookkeeping Study Manual and is ideal for students to use in the classroom, at home or on distance learning courses.

Each chapter contains exercises which are designed to supplement the activities in the Study Manual. Some of them are more extensive than those in the Study Manual and are ideal for students preparing for the examinations. Each chapter matches the topics in the Study Manual and can be attempted once the relevant chapter has been read. However, students should follow the chapters in order as some questions require the knowledge gained in previous chapters.

There are two practice examination papers at the end of the book. These should not be attempted until all the chapters have been read and understood. They are ideal preparation for the actual examination and should be attempted in the few weeks approaching the examination sitting date.

The answers to the Revision Kit questions and the practice examinations are given at the end of the book.

Premier Training students have online access to many extra resources which provides many further explanations and demonstrations of these and other topics. Visit www.premiertraining.co.uk or telephone 01469 515444.

Chapter 1

Accounting Roles and Transactions

1.1

Traditionally, is a bookkeeper, an accountant or an accounting technician more likely to complete the following?

a) Recording what sales have been made in the day
b) Recording what a company owns and what a company owes in a Balance Sheet
c) Money paid into and money paid from the bank on a day to day basis
d) A record of how much profit or loss a company has made in a year in a Profit and Loss statement
e) A report to the directors on whether to buy a new machine for £1,000,000

1.2

Explain

a) A sole trader
b) A partnership
c) A limited company

in terms of ownership and liability for debts

1.3

a) You work as an accounting technician. You have a number of colleagues all having different roles but responsible to the same department manager. The department manager is responsible directly to the managing director.

What organisational structure is the company most likely to have?

b) You work as an accounting technician. Your best friend works in the same company but in a different office with a different boss. However, the bosses in both offices work for the same Assistant Finance Director. The factory across the road has its own set of workers responsible to an Assistant Production Manager. The office block along the road is where the Director of Finance works. He liaises regularly with the Production Manager, the Sales Manager and the Buying Manager. Each of these is then responsible to the Board of Directors with the Chief Executive Officer in overall charge.

What organisational structure is the company most likely to have?

c) You work as an accounting technician. There are only two departments in your company, Finance and Production. You started as an office junior and have now worked your way up through junior accounts assistant to accounts assistant. You are now responsible for two junior accounts assistants and you in turn are responsible to the accounts office manager. The accounts office manager is hoping for a promotion to Assistant Financial Controller. Above the Assistant Financial Controller is the Financial Controller herself, who in turn is responsible to the Company Accountant. There are two directors who are in charge of the whole business.

What organisational structure is the company most likely to have?

d) You work as an accounting technician. Your company has branches in the UK, USA and Japan. It makes five different products which are in no way related. Apart from organising the structure on a functional basis, what other options does the company have for its organisational structure?

1.4

Explain what the following are

a) An invoice

b) A receipt

c) A public sector company

d) A shareholder

e) A book of prime entry.

Chapter 2

Selling Goods and Services

2.1

Explain the difference between a quote and an estimate.

2.2

Put these documents in the order they would be used in a sale.

- Invoice
- Advice Note
- Delivery Note
- Quotation
- Purchase Order

2.3

You buy your goods from the same supplier because the supplier offers a discount when you spend over £100. Is this likely to be:

a) A trade discount
b) A cash discount
c) A bulk discount?

2.4

You have received orders for coffee mugs you sell to the trade. These sell for £3.50 each.

K O'Brian has ordered 25
L Armstrong has ordered 50
H Wells has ordered 100
C Perry has ordered 60
J Booth has ordered 75

H Wells and J Booth are given a trade discount of 10%

Calculate the net totals before VAT.

2.5

Calculate the VAT (@20%) and the final totals for the amounts charged in task 2.4.

2.6

You are reminded that all the customers in task 2.4 are due a 2.5% settlement discount if the invoice is paid within 10 days. Recalculate the VAT amount and the total to account for this.

2.7

How much would each customer in task 2.4, 2.5 and 2.6 pay if they each paid within the 10 days?

2.8

You have three purchase orders shown on the next pages. You are to complete invoices for these orders. Use the blank invoices provided. Today's date is 1st June 2015 and the invoices should be in sequence starting with number 35279.

You should note that J Harper is allowed a 10% trade discount and that T Sawyer is allowed a 10% trade discount and is also offered a 2.5% settlement discount if the invoice is paid within 10 days.

H Finn

35 Buchanan Place, Peterhead, AB42 7RG

PURCHASE ORDER

Dawson Supplies
43 Scartho Road
Immingham
DN20 6NP

Invoice Address: 35 Buchanan Place
Peterhead
AB42 7RG

Delivery Address: 35 Buchanan Place
Peterhead
AB42 7RG

Purchase Order No: 4278

Order Date: 29th May 2015

Part Code	Qty	Description	Unit Price	Total Price
	100	Speciality Coffee Mugs	£3.50	£350.00
			Purchase Order Total:	**£350.00**

Authorised : *H Finn*   Date   *29/05/2015*

All orders are raised subject to our Terms and Conditions of trade. A full copy is available on request.
E&OE. All prices exclude VAT.

J Harper

67 David Street, Barry, CF63 2PQ

PURCHASE ORDER

Dawson Supplies
43 Scartho Road
Immingham
DN20 6NP

Invoice Address: 67 David Street   **Delivery Address:**   67 David Street
Barry   Barry
CF63 2PQ   CF63 2PQ

Purchase Order No: 3675

Order Date: 29th May 2015

Part Code	Qty	Description	Unit Price	Total Price
	150	Speciality Coffee Mugs	£3.50	£525.00

			Purchase Order Total:	**£525.00**

Authorised :   *J Harper*   Date   *29/05/2015*

All orders are raised subject to our Terms and Conditions of trade. A full copy is available on request.
E&OE. All prices exclude VAT.

T Sawyer

157 Patrick Street, Newry, BT34 9RY

PURCHASE ORDER

Dawson Supplies
43 Scartho Road
Immingham
DN20 6NP

Invoice Address: 157 Patrick Street
Newry
BT34 9RY

Delivery Address: 157 Patrick Street
Newry
BT34 9RY

Purchase Order No: 19735

Order Date: 29th May 2015

Part Code	Qty	Description	Unit Price	Total Price
	144	Speciality Coffee Mugs	£3.50	£504.00
			Purchase Order Total:	**£504.00**

Authorised : *T Sawyer*   Date   *29/05/2015*

All orders are raised subject to our Terms and Conditions of trade. A full copy is available on request.
E&OE. All prices exclude VAT.

DAWSON SUPPLIES

45 Scartho Street, Immingham, IM15 2BH

Invoice

Number:

Invoice to

Date/ tax point:

Account:

Your reference:

Deliver to

VAT
Reg: GB 369 4928 36

Product Code	Item	Quantity	Price £	Total £
Goods Total				
Trade Discount @ _____%				
Subtotal				
VAT @ 20%				
Invoice Total				

Terms
COD
Ex-works
E&OE

DAWSON SUPPLIES

45 Scartho Street, Immingham, IM15 2BH

Invoice

Number:

Invoice
to

Date/ tax point:

Account:

Your reference:

Deliver
to

VAT
Reg: GB 369 4928 36

Product Code	Item	Quantity	Price £	Total £
Goods Total				
Trade Discount @ _____%				
Subtotal				
VAT @ 20%				
Invoice Total				

Terms
COD
Ex-works
E&OE

DAWSON SUPPLIES

45 Scartho Street, Immingham, IM15 2BH

Invoice

Number:

Invoice
to

Date/ tax point:

Account:

Your reference:

Deliver
to

VAT
Reg: GB 369 4928 36

Product Code	Item	Quantity	Price £	Total £
Goods Total				
Trade Discount @ _____%				
Subtotal				
VAT @ 20%				
Invoice Total				

Terms
COD
Ex-works
E&OE

10

2.9

Following from task 2.8, T Sawyer has found that 12 of the mugs were damaged when he received them. You have agreed that a credit note can be issued for the damaged mugs. They have been returned and you have a signed returns note for the goods. You are to complete the following credit note. Today's date is 5th June 2015 and the next credit note number is CN357.

DAWSON SUPPLIES

45 Scartho Street, Immingham, IM15 2BH

Credit Note

Number:

To

Date/ tax point:

Account:

Your reference:

VAT Reg: GB 369 4928 36

Our invoice no.

Product Code	Item	Quantity	Price £	Total £
Goods Total				
Trade Discount @ ____%				
Subtotal				
VAT @ 20%				
Credit Total				

Reason for Credit

2.10

At the beginning of June 2015 T Sawyer had an opening balance of £525.00.

He bought the goods invoiced in task 2.8.

On 4th June he paid £513.83 which was for the opening balance, but which he took £11.17 settlement discount to which he was entitled.

On 5th June the credit note in task 2.9 was sent.

On 8th June he paid £486.48 which was in respect of invoice 35281 and credit note CN357. T Sawyer took the settlement discount to which he was entitled.

On 26th June he bought more goods. The invoice total was £75.85 (Invoice 35396)

Draw up T Sawyer's statement of account for 30th June.

STATEMENT OF ACCOUNT
Dawson Supplies

154 Margaret St, Immingham, IM17 9RQ

To

Account

Date

Date	Details	Debit £	Credit £	Balance £

TOTAL AMOUNT OUTSTANDING

Chapter 3

VAT and Legal Considerations

3.1

In preparation for completing the VAT return, you have the following invoices and till receipts. You are required to list the VAT elements of each invoice

a)   Invoice from a supplier (VAT number GB 233 2396 84)
        Subtotal £250.00   VAT amount   £50.00   Total £300.00

b)   Invoice from window cleaner (No VAT number)
        Total amount £25.00

c)   Receipt from local shop for stationery (VAT number GB 375 9651 29)
        Total amount £26.22

d)   Receipt for tea and coffee from local shop (VAT number GB 339 2467 32)
        Total amount £17.50.

e)   Invoice from a supplier (VAT number GB 796 4359 14)
        Subtotal £605.00   VAT amount £112.00   Total £717.00

3.2

Read the following scenario.

Hannah goes to her favourite department store. It's January and the sales are on. She sees the latest fashions all at reduced prices. Eventually she chooses an elegant red evening dress advertised on the stand at £150, reduced from £350.

She manages to push past the crowds to the counter with her selection and stands patiently in the queue. Eventually she gets to the front of the queue, places the dress on the counter and gets out her credit card. The checkout girl rings it through the till and wraps the article of clothing and places it in a bag.

Hannah gets home and eagerly puts on the dress only to find that the size shown on the label is not the size of the dress. Hannah has been a size 14 for years and in spite of the label, she estimates that this dress can be no more than a size 10.

Disappointedly, she puts the dress back in the bag and makes the trip back to the shop hoping for a refund. When she gets to the customer services counter they ask for her receipt, but to her dismay it's not in the bag. She must have lost it somewhere between the shop and home. The salesperson says that regrettably there can be no refunds without a receipt.

Hannah leaves the shop with her unwearable dress £150 poorer.

Required:

1) Identify the offer in this scenario.

2) Identify the acceptance.

3) Identify the consideration provided by both sides.

4) Discuss whether Hannah is entitled to a refund.

5) Discuss whether the salesperson is correct to say 'no refunds without a receipt'.

3.3

Read the following scenario.

Toby has hired a plumber to fit a new bathroom suite. It has been agreed that the plumber comes on Tuesday so Toby has booked a day off work so that he can be at home while the plumber fits the suite.

Toby is expecting the plumber at 8.30am but at 10.30am there is still no sign of the plumber. Eventually at 11.00am Toby gets a phone call from the plumber. His vehicle has broken down and will not be able to get to Toby's house that day.

The plumber tells Toby that he will still do the job, but he won't be able to book Toby in for two weeks. Toby can't wait for two weeks so he tells the plumber he will get someone else to do the job. The plumber says he understands and apologises for the inconvenience.

Does a contract still exist?

If not then how has it been discharged?

3.4

Under the Sale of Goods Act, what are your rights in respect of faulty goods if you are:

a)   A Sole Trader

b)   A member of the public who is the end user of the goods?

Chapter 4

Recording Sales and Sales Returns

4.1

What is an integrated ledger?

4.2

Give an example of each of the following

    a) Prime document

    b) Book of Prime Entry

    c) A Ledger

4.3

You work for BBJ Sports, supplying sports goods to the retail trade. The following credit sales were made during May 2015. Enter the sales in the Sales day Book. (VAT is charged at 20%). Total the Sales Day Book for the month.

May 1st	10 pairs dumbbells to L Walsh	£10 each plus VAT	Invoice 36597
May 4th	5 tennis rackets to C Cole	£80 each plus VAT	Invoice 36598
May 8th	12 punch bags to S Cowell	£25 each plus VAT	Invoice 36599
May 15th	24 footballs to D O'Leary	£7.50 each plus VAT	Invoice 36600
May 18th	1 set golf clubs to D Minogue	£250 set plus VAT	Invoice 36601
May 22nd	24 snooker cues to L Walsh	£4 each plus VAT	Invoice 36602
May 25th	6 cricket balls to D O'Leary	£2 each plus VAT	Invoice 36603
May 29th	12 basketballs to L Walsh	£5 each plus VAT	Invoice 36604

C Cole account is SL 08   D Minogue account is SL 58
S Cowell account is SL 12   O'Leary account is SL 72
L Walsh account is SL 97

SALES DAY BOOK **SDB 97**

Date	Invoice	Customer	Folio	Total		Sales		VAT	
				£	p	£	p	£	p
		TOTAL FOR THE MONTH							

4.4

Using the answers for task 4.3, post the Sales Day Book to the Main Ledger accounts and the individual customer accounts. The accounts are shown on p18-p20.

4.5

The following Credit Notes were issued in the same month. Enter these in the Sales Returns Day Book.

2015
11th May   S Cowell returned 1 punch bag as it was faulty   CN75
18th May   D O'Leary returned 2 footballs as they were faulty   CN76

Date	Cr Note	Customer	Folio	Total		Sales		VAT	
				£	p	£	p	£	p
		TOTAL FOR THE MONTH							

SALES RETURNS DAY BOOK   **SRDB 12**

4.6

Using the answers for task 4.5, post the Sales Returns Day Book to the Main Ledger accounts and the individual customer accounts. Use the accounts already prepared in task 4.4.

4.7

Balance all the accounts.

4.8

Reconcile the Sales Ledger Control account to the Sales Ledger accounts.

Reconciliation of Sales Ledger Control Account
31st May 2015

	£	£
L Walsh		
C Cole		
S Cowell		
D O'Leary		
D Minogue	_____	
TOTAL		
TOTAL PER SALES LEDGER CONTROL		
Discrepancy (if any)	_____	

SALES LEDGER

Dr	L Walsh Account (SL 97)				Cr
Date	Details	£	Date	Details	£

Dr	C Cole Account (SL 08)				Cr
Date	Details	£	Date	Details	£

Dr	S Cowell Account (SL 12)				Cr
Date	Details	£	Date	Details	£

Dr	D O'Leary Account (SL 72)				Cr
Date	Details	£	Date	Details	£

Dr	D Minogue Account (SL 58)				Cr
Date	Details	£	Date	Details	£

MAIN LEDGER

Dr	Sales Account (4000)				Cr
Date	Details	£	Date	Details	£

Dr	Sales Returns Account (4050)				Cr
Date	Details	£	Date	Details	£

Dr			VAT Account (2200)		Cr
Date	Details	£	Date	Details	£

Dr			Sales Ledger Control Account (1100)		Cr
Date	Details	£	Date	Details	£

Chapter 5

Cash Receipts and Cash Sales

5.1

Thrushcross Ltd keeps an analysed cash book. Money received is entered into the cash book and at the end of the day it is totalled and posted to the main ledger accounts. Thrushcross Ltd does not have a separate bank account and so the cash book is part of the main ledger. Money is banked at the end of each day which means a separate cash column is not required. (The current rate of VAT is 20%).

The opening balance on 4th May 2015 was £1760.00.

The following transactions took place on 4th May 2015:

Cash sale (including VAT). The customer paid by cheque.   £257.40

Received BACS advice for £565.50 from C Earnshaw in full settlement of her account of £580.00

Cash sale (including VAT). The customer paid by cheque.   £210.00

 Interest on a loan to N Dean was received (no VAT)   £60.00

Cash sale (including VAT) paid in cash   £108.00

Rent received from a tenant E Linton (no VAT)   £300.00

Cash sale (including VAT). The customer paid by cash   £60.00

R Lockwood settles an invoice for £796.65 paying £779.70; the balance being the settlement discount.

Cash sale (including VAT). The customer paid by cheque   £69.60

J Heathcliffe settles his invoice for £881.25 by cheque

Enter these transactions into the analysed cash book on the next page and then total the columns

The accounts are:

C Earnshaw   SL25   R Lockwood   SL72
J Heathcliffe   SL32

CASHBOOK - RECEIPTS — CBR96

Date	Detail	Folio	Discount Allowed		Bank		Cash Sale		VAT		Sales Ledger		Other Income	
			£	p	£	p	£	p	£	p	£	p	£	p

5.2

Post the cash book totals you calculated in Task 5.1 to the main ledger accounts and the subsidiary ledger accounts. You are not required to show opening balances or to balance any accounts.

SALES LEDGER

Dr	C Earnshaw Account (SL 25)				Cr
Date	Details	£	Date	Details	£

Dr	J Heathcliffe Account (SL 32)				Cr
Date	Details	£	Date	Details	£

Dr	R Lockwood Account (SL 72)				Cr
Date	Details	£	Date	Details	£

MAIN LEDGER

Dr	Sales Account (4000)				Cr
Date	Details	£	Date	Details	£

Dr	Interest Received Account (4902)				Cr
Date	Details	£	Date	Details	£

Dr	Rent Received Account (4904)				Cr
Date	Details	£	Date	Details	£

Dr	VAT Account (2200)				Cr
Date	Details	£	Date	Details	£

Dr	Sales Ledger Control Account (1100)				Cr
Date	Details	£	Date	Details	£

Dr	Discounts Allowed Account (4009)				Cr
Date	Details	£	Date	Details	£

5.3

a)   A customer writes out the following cheques. She wants to buy some DIY goods from your company, C&R, which come to a total of £350.00, but the cheque guarantee card is for only £200.00. Today's date is 5th May 2015.

LINCOLN BANK plc		30 - 71 – 69
75 Portland Place, Lincoln, LN2 1ET		

Date   *5th May 2015*

Pay   *C&R Ltd*

Two Hundred Pounds   A/C Payee   *Only*   £   *200.00*

L Butler

L Butler

Cheque number	Sort Code	Account number
500175	30-71-69	23978621

| LINCOLN BANK plc | | | | 30 - 71 - 69 |
| 75 Portland Place, Lincoln, LN2 1ET | | | | |

Date *5th May 2015*

Pay *C&R Ltd*

One Hundred and Fifty Pounds **£** *150.00*

only *L Butler*

| Cheque number | Sort Code | Account number | L Butler |
| 500176 | 30-71-69 | 23978621 | |

What action would you take and why?

b)   You receive the following cheque by post. It is from D Wakefield, a credit customer, in payment of his outstanding invoice. It is 5th May 2015.

| WILLIAMS BANK plc | | | | 09 – 36 – 21 |
| 14 St Martins Square, Swindon, SN1 6TY | | | | |

Date

Pay *C&R Ltd*

Fifty Pounds only   ------   **£** *50.00*

-------------------------   *D Wakefield*

| Cheque number | Sort Code | Account number | D Wakefield |
| 001482 | 09-36-21 | 29658737 | |

What action would you take and why?

c)   You receive the following cheque by post. It is from J Powell, a credit customer, in payment of her outstanding invoice. It is 5th May 2015.

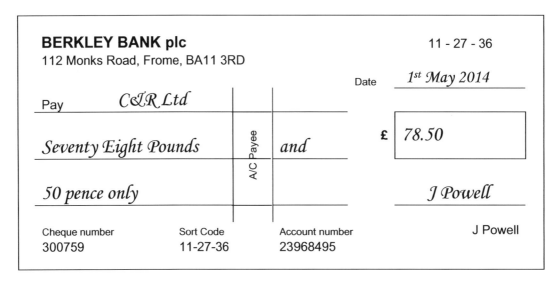

What action would you take and why?

d)   What do the crossings (two vertical lines with the words A/C Payee) mean on the above cheques?

5.4

Explain the difference between a cheque and a banker's draft.

Chapter 6

Dealing with Banks

6.1

You work for D&R Ltd. Your company sells soft furnishings to the general public through a small retail shop. Customers pay for their goods by cash, cheque, debit card or credit card. Each morning the shop till starts with a float of £50, (kept in a locked cash box and taken home by the proprietor each evening).

The float consists of

Six £5 notes 30
Ten £1 coins 10
Five 50p coins 2.50
Twenty 20p coins 4
Twenty 10p coins 2
Twenty 5p coins 1
Twenty 2p coins .40
Ten 1p coins .10

One of your daily tasks is to count up the cash in the till and prepare a paying-in slip ready for payment to the bank. The following table shows the notes and coins counted from the till. You are to complete the table and say how much money was taken in the day.

Denomination	Quantity	Total £
£50	0	
£20	7	
£10	15	
£5	11	
£1	25	
50p	5	
20p	45	
10p	52	
5p	25	
2p	36	
1p	11	

6.2

In addition to the notes and coins counted in task 6.1 there were two cheques.

From D Ryder   £175.00

From G Coulter   £225.00

Prepare the front and rear of the paying-in slip. (Today is 6th May 2015).

Date				Please detail cheques and slips on the back
Cashier's stamp		**Bank Giro Credit**	£50	
		IMMINGHAM BANK plc	£20	
		14 Springfield Road, Brigg, DN20 3GF	£10	
		Account	£5	
		D&R Ltd	£1	
NUMBER OF CHEQUES/ SLIPS		**Paid in by**	50p	
			Silver	
			Bronze	
			TOTAL CASH	
			Cheque/slips	
		Sort Code Account Number	£	
		01-26-73 54379654		

Paying in slip (front)

Details of cheques/slips	Amount	
	£	p
Total cheques/slips carried over		

Paying in slip (back)

6.3

Explain the following relationships between a customer and a bank

a)   Debtor and Creditor

b)   Bailor and Bailee

c)   Mortgagor and Mortgagee

d)   Principal and Agent

6.4

Briefly explain why you can't draw money on a cheque as soon as you put it in the bank.

6.5

Give 5 security measures when handling cash.

Chapter 7

Recording Purchases

7.1

Today is 5th May 2015. You work for GiftsRHere which sells a selection of gift items from a local store. You receive the following invoices from your credit suppliers.

Invoice 53798 from I Fleming   6 Jewellery Boxes £86.40 including VAT
Invoice 36742 from T Hardy   12 Candle Holders £360.00 including VAT
Invoice 2579 from A Huxley   24 Photo Frames £345.60 including VAT
Invoice 36821 from E Waugh   1 refill cartridge for office printer £15.00 inc VAT
Invoice 68687 from D Lawrence   10 Glass Vases £90.00 including VAT
Invoice 35761 from P Wodehouse   5 Bread Bins £87.00 including VAT

Purchases Ledger account numbers

I Fleming	PL 17	D Lawrence	PL 46
T Hardy	PL 21	E Waugh	PL 58
A Huxley	PL 23	P Wodehouse	PL 61

Enter the transactions into the purchases day book on the next page
Total the purchases day book
Post the entries to the main and subsidiary ledgers on the following pages

7.2

It is now 7th May 2015. You receive the following credit notes

Credit Note CN 132 from A Huxley 1 Photo Frame (damaged) £14.40 including VAT
Credit Note C 268 from D Lawrence 1 Glass Vase (chipped) £9.00 including VAT

Enter the transactions into the purchases returns day book
Total the purchases returns day book and post the entries into the same accounts you used for task 7.1

Balance the accounts. Today's date is 8th May 2015.

PURCHASES DAY BOOK PDB 36

Date	Invoice	Supplier	Folio	Total		Purchases		Other expenses		VAT	
				£	p	£	p	£	p	£	p
		TOTAL									

PURCHASES RETURNS DAY BOOK PRDB 05

Date	Cr Note	Supplier	Folio	Total		Purchases returns		Other returns		VAT	
				£	p	£	p	£	p	£	p
		TOTAL									

PURCHASES LEDGER

Dr	I Fleming Account (PL 17)				Cr
Date	Details	£	Date	Details	£

Dr	T Hardy Account (PL 21)				Cr
Date	Details	£	Date	Details	£

Dr	A Huxley Account (PL 23)				Cr
Date	Details	£	Date	Details	£

Dr	D Lawrence Account (PL 46)				Cr
Date	Details	£	Date	Details	£

Dr	E Waugh Account (PL 58)				Cr
Date	Details	£	Date	Details	£

Dr	P Wodehouse Account (PL 61)				Cr
Date	Details	£	Date	Details	£

MAIN LEDGER

Dr		Purchases			Cr
Date	Details	£	Date	Details	£

Dr		Purchases Returns			Cr
Date	Details	£	Date	Details	£

Dr		Other expenses			Cr
Date	Details	£	Date	Details	£

Dr		VAT Account			Cr
Date	Details	£	Date	Details	£

Dr		Purchases Ledger Control Account			Cr
Date	Details	£	Date	Details	£

Chapter 8

Making Payments

8.1

You work for 'CDs for you'. The main ledger contains the following accounts on 1st June 2015.

Purchases   balance £23,567.57 debit
Purchases Returns   balance £2026.35 credit
VAT   balance £1884.85 credit

The subsidiary purchases ledger contains the following balances on 1st June 2015.

E Corney (PL 27)   balance £375.92
F Bumble (PL 06)   balance £1,672.57
E Leeford (PL 45)   balance £1,007.63
W Sikes (PL 68)   balance £257.92
C Bedwin (PL 03)   balance £654.87
N Claypole (PL 23)   balance £329.64

The following transactions took place and were authorised during June 2015. 'CDs for you' gives a unique number to each invoice and credit note as it is received.

1st June	Bought goods on credit from W Sikes for £150.00 + VAT, inv 2345
5th June	Bought goods on credit from E Corney for £375.00 + VAT, inv 2346
8th June	Returned goods to C Bedwin £75.00 + VAT, credit note 17
12th June	Bought goods on credit from E Corney for £450.00 + VAT, inv 2347
15th June	Bought goods on credit from E Leeford for £325.00 + VAT, inv 2348
19th June	Bought goods on credit from C Bedwin for £210.00 + VAT, inv 2349
22nd June	Returned goods to F Bumble £115.00 + VAT, credit note 18
23rd June	Bought goods on credit from N Claypole for £750.00 + VAT, inv 2350
26th June	Bought goods on credit from W Sikes for £250.00 + VAT, inv 2351
29th June	Returned goods to N Claypole £50.00 + VAT, credit note 19
30th June	Transfer debit balance of £822.50 in subsidiary sales ledger to F Bumble's account in the subsidiary purchases ledger

You are to

(a)   Prepare accounts in the main ledger and the subsidiary purchases ledger of 'CDs for you' at 1st June 2015

(b)   Enter the transactions into the purchases day book and the purchases returns day book.

(c)   From the books of prime entry, post the entries for June in the main ledger and the subsidiary purchases ledger (including the set-off). Balance the accounts at 30th June 2015.

(d)   Reconcile the control account balance with the subsidiary accounts at 1st June and 30th June 2015.

PURCHASES DAY BOOK   **PDB 36**

Date	Invoice	Customer	Folio	Total		Purchases		Other expenses		VAT	
				£	p	£	p	£	p	£	p
		TOTAL									

PURCHASES RETURNS DAY BOOK   PRDB 05

Date	Cr Note	Customer	Folio	Total		Purchases returns		Other returns		VAT	
				£	p	£	p	£	p	£	p
		TOTAL									

PURCHASES LEDGER

Dr			C Bedwin Account (PL 03)		Cr
Date	Details	£	Date	Details	£

Dr			F Bumble Account (PL 06)		Cr
Date	Details	£	Date	Details	£

Dr			N Claypole Account (PL 23)		Cr
Date	Details	£	Date	Details	£

Dr	E Corney Account (PL 27)				Cr
Date	Details	£	Date	Details	£

Dr	E Leeford Account (PL 45)				Cr
Date	Details	£	Date	Details	£

Dr	W Sikes Account (PL 68)				Cr
Date	Details	£	Date	Details	£

MAIN LEDGER

Dr	Purchases				Cr
Date	Details	£	Date	Details	£

Dr	Purchases Returns				Cr
Date	Details	£	Date	Details	£

Dr	VAT Account				Cr
Date	Details	£	Date	Details	£

Dr	Purchases Ledger Control Account				Cr
Date	Details	£	Date	Details	£

Reconciliation of Purchases Ledger Control Account
30th June 2015

	£	£
C Bedwin		
F Bumble		
N Claypole		
E Corney		
E Leeford		
W Sikes		
TOTAL		
TOTAL PER PURCHASES LEDGER CONTROL		
Discrepancy (if any)		

8.2

You have returned from holiday and find that payments to suppliers have been overlooked. It is company policy to pay strictly to the terms of the invoice and take advantage of any settlement discount offered.

Today is 29th June 2015. The company writes cheques to suppliers once a week.

A summary of the invoices is given below:

Invoice Date	Supplier	Terms	Net	VAT	Invoice Total
			£	£	£
15th May	A Haig	60 days	450.00	90.00	540.00
29th May	D MacArthur	30 days	255.00	51.00	306.00
1st June	G Patton	30 days	275.00	55.00	330.00
5th June	R Lee	30 days	350.00	70.00	420.00
12th June	C Gordon	30 days*	1050.00	204.75	1254.75
15th June	J Pershing	30 days	110.00	22.00	132.00
18th June	T Jackson	30 days	240.00	48.00	288.00
24th June	W Sherman	30 days*	950.00	185.25	1135.25
26th June	B Montgomery	30 days	400.00	80.00	480.00

*These invoices have a 2.5% settlement discount for payment within 7 days.

You are to complete the cheques for those which require payment. You are not to sign the cheques as these will be authorised and signed by your supervisor later.

IMMINGHAM BANK plc
14 Springfield Road, Brigg, DN20 3GF

30 - 25 - 81

Date _____

Pay _____

A/C Payee

£ _____

Cheque number
001481

Sort Code
30-25-81

Account number
12560798

S Craggs

IMMINGHAM BANK plc

14 Springfield Road, Brigg, DN20 3GF

30 - 25 - 81

Date _____

Pay _____

A/C Payee

£ _____

Cheque number   Sort Code   Account number
001482   30-25-81   12560798

S Craggs

IMMINGHAM BANK plc

14 Springfield Road, Brigg, DN20 3GF

30 - 25 - 81

Date _____

Pay _____

A/C Payee

£ _____

Cheque number   Sort Code   Account number
001483   30-25-81   12560798

S Craggs

IMMINGHAM BANK plc

14 Springfield Road, Brigg, DN20 3GF

30 - 25 - 81

Date _____

Pay _____

A/C Payee

£ _____

Cheque number   Sort Code   Account number
001484   30-25-81   12560798

S Craggs

IMMINGHAM BANK plc

14 Springfield Road, Brigg, DN20 3GF

30 - 25 - 81

Date

Pay

A/C Payee

£

Cheque number	Sort Code	Account number
001485	30-25-81	12560798

S Craggs

IMMINGHAM BANK plc

14 Springfield Road, Brigg, DN20 3GF

30 - 25 - 81

Date

Pay

A/C Payee

£

Cheque number	Sort Code	Account number
001486	30-25-81	12560798

S Craggs

IMMINGHAM BANK plc

14 Springfield Road, Brigg, DN20 3GF

30 - 25 - 81

Date

Pay

A/C Payee

£

Cheque number	Sort Code	Account number
001487	30-25-81	12560798

S Craggs

IMMINGHAM BANK plc

14 Springfield Road, Brigg, DN20 3GF

30 - 25 - 81

Date _____

Pay _____

A/C Payee

£ [   ]

_____

_____

| Cheque number | Sort Code | Account number | S Craggs |
| 001488 | 30-25-81 | 12560798 | |

IMMINGHAM BANK plc

14 Springfield Road, Brigg, DN20 3GF

30 - 25 - 81

Date _____

Pay _____

A/C Payee

£ [   ]

_____

_____

| Cheque number | Sort Code | Account number | S Craggs |
| 001489 | 30-25-81 | 12560798 | |

8.3

You work for a clothes retailer 'Casuals'. The following transactions took place last week (Week commencing 1st June 2015).

1st June	Cash purchase of £150.00 including VAT. Paid by cheque No 6735
1st June	Paid C Dior, a creditor, £286.40, taking a discount of £6.25. Cheque no 6736
2nd June	Bought stationery for £30.00 including VAT. Cheque no 6737
2nd June	Paid D Dolce, a creditor, £552.25. Paid by cheque No 6738
2nd June	Paid rent, £450.00 (no VAT). Cheque no 6739
3rd June	Paid S Gabbana, a creditor, £630.09. A discount of £13.75 was taken. Cheque no 6740
4th June	Made a cash purchase of £96.00 including VAT. Cheque no 6741
5th June	Bought tea and coffee for the office £9.60 (no VAT). Cheque no 6742

5th June   Paid C Klein, a creditor, £996.69. A discount of £21.75 was taken. Cheque no 6743.

5th June   Paid wages of £1765.36 (no VAT) by BACS.

Show the entries in the cash book (payments side). Total the columns and post the amounts to the appropriate accounts. (You are not required to show any opening balances or balance any accounts)

CASHBOOK - PAYMENTS   **CBP83**

Date	Detail	Discount Received		Bank		Cash Purchases		VAT		Purchases Ledger		Other Expenses	
		£	p	£	p	£	p	£	p	£	p	£	p

PURCHASES LEDGER

Dr			C Dior Account		Cr
Date	Details	£	Date	Details	£

44

Dr	D Dolce Account				Cr
Date	Details	£	Date	Details	£

Dr	S Gabbana Account				Cr
Date	Details	£	Date	Details	£

Dr	C Klein Account				Cr
Date	Details	£	Date	Details	£

MAIN LEDGER

Dr	Purchases				Cr
Date	Details	£	Date	Details	£

Dr	Other expenses				Cr
Date	Details	£	Date	Details	£

Dr	VAT Account				Cr
Date	Details	£	Date	Details	£

Dr	Purchases Ledger Control Account				Cr
Date	Details	£	Date	Details	£

Dr	Discounts Received Account				Cr
Date	Details	£	Date	Details	£

Chapter 9

Petty Cash

9.1

The company operates the imprest system and keeps an imprest amount of £200.00. You have totalled the analysis columns for the week and they show:

VAT   £12.24
Travel   £50.50
Stationery £29.50
Postage   £19.36
Sundry   £15.45

How much will you need to draw from the bank to restore the imprest amount?

9.2

You work in a small restaurant where it is part of your duties to pay and record petty cash amounts. The company operates the imprest system and keeps an imprest amount of £200.00. The maximum that can be drawn on any one transaction is £50.

Below are the receipts you have received during the week commencing 1st June 2015. You are to write the petty cash vouchers for those claims you are satisfied with. Remember that VAT is not charged on postage or train travel. You should give a new number to each voucher beginning with 0698 and sign the authorisation. (You may assume that all expenses are for business purposes). Today's date is 6th June 2015.

| **Spondon Post Office** |
| Chapel St, Spondon |
| DE21 6LE |
| VAT Reg 491 3267 20 |

Stamps	£8.50
Amount tendered	£10.00
Change	£1.50
Date	1st June 2015

| **Dave's Taxis** |
| 75 High Street, |
| Borrowash |
| DE72 5RZ |
| Tel: 01332 232 232 |

| Date | *2nd June 2015* |
| Received with thanks | *£5.70* |

VAT Reg 491 3267 20

National Trains
Railway Street,
Derby
DE1 8UY
Tel : 0845 637 4920

TRAIN TICKET RECEIPT

Amount   *£32.00*

Date   *2nd June 2015*

National Trains - We're going places

Spondon Office Supplies
36 Vine Street, Spondon
DE21 1LE
VAT Reg 697 4351 01
03-06-2015

Goods   £34.80

Amount Tendered   £40.00

Change   £5.20

The above goods include VAT @ 20%

Spondon Post Office
Chapel St, Spondon
DE21 6LE
VAT Reg 491 3267 20

Parcel Postage   £15.60

Amount tendered   £20.00

Change   £4.40

Date   3rd June 2015

Dave's Taxis
75 High Street,
Borrowash
DE72 5RZ
Tel: 01332 232 232

Date   *3rd June 2015*

Received with thanks   *£7.50*

VAT Reg 491 3267 20

DERBY OFFICE PRINTERS
15 Lincoln Road, DERBY
DE21 6ME
VAT Reg 470 6329 50
04-06-2015

Laser Copier Cartridge   £59.99

Amount Tendered   £60.00

Change   £0.01

The above goods include VAT @ 20%

Dave's Taxis
75 High Street,
Borrowash
DE72 5RZ
Tel: 01332 232 232

Date   *5th June 2015*

Received with thanks   *£4.50*

VAT Reg 491 3267 20

Petty Cash Voucher	No
Date prepared	
Expenditure	**Amount (£)**
VAT	
TOTAL	£
Paid to	_____
Authorised	_____

Petty Cash Voucher	No
Date prepared	
Expenditure	**Amount (£)**
VAT	
TOTAL	£
Paid to	_____
Authorised	_____

Petty Cash Voucher	No
Date prepared	
Expenditure	**Amount (£)**
VAT	
TOTAL	£
Paid to	_____
Authorised	_____

Petty Cash Voucher	No
Date prepared	
Expenditure	**Amount (£)**
VAT	
TOTAL	£
Paid to	_____
Authorised	_____

Petty Cash Voucher	No
Date prepared	
Expenditure	**Amount (£)**
VAT	
TOTAL	**£**
Paid to	_____
Authorised	_____

Petty Cash Voucher	No
Date prepared	
Expenditure	**Amount (£)**
VAT	
TOTAL	**£**
Paid to	_____
Authorised	_____

Petty Cash Voucher   **No**

Date prepared

Expenditure	Amount (£)
VAT	
TOTAL	£

Paid to   _____

Authorised   _____

Petty Cash Voucher   **No**

Date prepared

Expenditure	Amount (£)
VAT	
TOTAL	£

Paid to   _____

Authorised   _____

9.3

Write up the petty cash book for the week commencing 1st June 2015. The petty cash started with an imprest balance of £200. Record the petty cash vouchers you have authorised.

Total the columns and restore the imprest with a transfer from the cash book.

Balance the petty cash book as at 6th June 2015 and bring down a balance on 7th June 2015.

Petty Cash Book															PCB45
Receipts		Date	Detail	Voucher Number	Total		Analysis Columns								
							VAT		Travel		Stationery		Postage		
£	p				£	p	£	p	£	p	£	p	£	p	

Chapter 10

Wages and Salaries

10.1

The following payroll totals are available for May 2015.

Gross pay	£60,000
Income Tax	£8,379
NIC Employee	£4,608
NIC Employer	£5,362
Pension Employee	£4,200
Pension Employer	£4,200

(a)   Calculate the total expense to the company

(b)   Calculate the total amount due to HMRC

(c)   Calculate the net pay due to the employees

(d)   Draw up the double entry in the following accounts

Dr	Wages Expense Account				Cr
Date	Details	£	Date	Details	£

Dr	Wages Control Account				Cr
Date	Details	£	Date	Details	£

Dr	Bank Account				Cr
Date	Details	£	Date	Details	£

Dr	HMRC Account				Cr
Date	Details	£	Date	Details	£

Dr	Pension Fund Account				Cr
Date	Details	£	Date	Details	£

10.2

The following table shows the hours worked for Ayesha Gupta during the week commencing 1st June 2015

	Monday	Tuesday	Wednesday	Thursday	Friday
Hours	8 hours	9 hours	10 hours 30 minutes	8 hours 45 minutes	9 hours 15 minutes

Ayesha is paid £12.00 per hour for 8 hours each day. If she works over the 8 hours each extra hour (or part of an hour) is paid at time and a half.

Calculate her total gross pay for the week.

Chapter 11

Methods of Communication

11.1

You work in a bicycle store 'Two Wheels' and you have received the following delivery note from your supplier 'On Your Bike' which you have checked against the purchase order (on the following page).

On Your Bike
127 St Martin's Street, Ipswich, IP1 6RQ

DELIVERY NOTE
NO. 26980

To :	Two Wheels	Your Order Number :	2398
Address :	37 South Street	Date Sent :	1st June 2015
	Salisbury	Per Invoice Number :	136749
	SP2 3EQ	Our Contact Person :	A Jamal
Attention :	V Symanski	Telephone :	01722 437589

Quantity Delivered	Description
2	Cruiser bicycles (blue)

Goods received in good order

Name :	V Symanski	Signature :	*V Symanski*	Date :	*1/6/15*

Two Wheels

37 South Street, Salisbury, SP2 3EQ

PURCHASE ORDER

On Your Bike
127 St Martin's Street
Ipswich
IP1 6RQ

Invoice Address: 37 South Street
Salisbury
SP2 3EQ

Delivery Address: 37 South Street
Salisbury
SP2 3EQ

Purchase Order No: 2398

Order Date 29th May 2015

Part Code	Qty	Description	Unit Price	Total Price
	2	Cruiser bicycles (red)	£410.00	£820.00

			Purchase Order Total:	£820.00

Authorised : *V Symanski*   Date   *29/05/2015*

All orders are raised subject to our Terms and Conditions of trade. A full copy is available on request.
E&OE. All prices exclude VAT.

Use the following headed paper to write a letter to the supplier, explaining what is wrong with the delivery. Use your own name and the title Accounts Assistant. Today's date is 2nd June 2015.

TWO WHEELS

37 South Street,
Salisbury,
SP2 3EQ

11.2

Send a memo to the stores manager to explain what has happened with the bikes from task 11.1. The stores manager is A Khan. Put the owner (V Symanski) on copy.

Memorandum

To:

cc:

From:

Date:

Re:

Chapter 12

Less Common Transactions

12.1

Your business is registered for VAT (current rate of 20%). The following transactions took place:

1st June 2015	Started business with £100,000 capital in the bank
1st June 2015	Bought office premises for £150,000 (Exempt from VAT)
2nd June 2015	Bought a Photocopier and Computer for a total of £1500 + VAT (show in office equipment account)
2nd June 2015	Received a loan from the bank for £100,000 (No VAT) (Show in the bank loan account)
3rd June 2015	Bought office fittings for £2,000 + VAT (Show in office fittings account)
3rd June 2015	Paid £450 + VAT for advertisement in daily paper
4th June 2015	Paid business rates £1000 (no VAT)
5th June 2015	Receive payment for letting of spare office space. £300 (no VAT)
5th June 2015	Took drawings of £350 from the bank
5th June 2015	Receive commission of £200 + VAT
5th June 2015	Repay some of the loan. £5000 (£192 interest; £4808 capital repayment)

You are to enter the above transactions into the appropriate accounts shown below. You do not need to balance any accounts at this stage.

CASH BOOK

RECEIPTS   PAYMENTS

Date	Detail	Bank £	Date	Detail	Bank £

Dr			Capital Account		Cr
Date	Details	£	Date	Details	£

Dr			VAT Account		Cr
Date	Details	£	Date	Details	£

Dr			Premises Account		Cr
Date	Details	£	Date	Details	£

Dr			Office Fittings Account		Cr
Date	Details	£	Date	Details	£

Dr			Office Equipment Account		Cr
Date	Details	£	Date	Details	£

Dr			Rates Account		Cr
Date	Details	£	Date	Details	£

60

Dr	Rent Receivable Account				Cr
Date	Details	£	Date	Details	£

Dr	Bank Loan Account				Cr
Date	Details	£	Date	Details	£

Dr	Advertising Account				Cr
Date	Details	£	Date	Details	£

Dr	Drawings Account				Cr
Date	Details	£	Date	Details	£

Dr	Commission Account				Cr
Date	Details	£	Date	Details	£

Dr	Interest Paid Account				Cr
Date	Details	£	Date	Details	£

12.2

Classify the following into either *capital expenditure* or *revenue expenditure*

	Capital Expenditure	Revenue Expenditure
Buying a new property		
Decoration of the new property		
Insurance of property		
Purchase of new Vehicle		
Annual Road Fund Licence for vehicle		
Fuel for Vehicle		
Repair of broken window		
Purchase of stock of goods for sale to customers		
Purchase of stock of copy paper for the photocopier		
New machine for the factory		
Delivery cost of the machine		
12 months service agreement on the machine		

12.3

A credit customer, Monkson Ltd., has ceased trading, owing your company £3,800 plus VAT. The net amount and the VAT must be written off in the main ledger. Show which accounts you would debit and which you would credit and the amount required in each. (Your company keeps individual accounts in a subsidiary ledger as memorandum accounts)

Account name	Debit £	Credit £
Bad Debt account		
VAT account		
Sales Ledger Control		

Do any other accounts need adjusting? Give reasons for your answer.

Chapter 13

The Cash Book and Bank Statement

13.1

You work for a building supplier 'M&J's'. The following transactions took place last month (June 2015):

1st June	Received cheque (No 35716) for £587.50 from F L Wright, a credit customer in full settlement of invoice 23698.
1st June	Paid C Wren, a creditor, £253.60, taking a discount of £6.40. Cheque no 2398
5th June	Bought stationery for £30.00 including VAT. Paid by cheque no 2399
8th June	Paid telephone bill, £174.32. Paid by cheque No 2400
12th June	Received cheque (No 42918) for £528.72 from J Nash, a credit customer in full settlement of invoice 23701
15th June	Paid C Barry, a creditor, £172.50, taking a discount of £3.75. Cheque no 2401
15th June	Received £58.79 in cash being settlement of invoice 23699
15th June	Received cheque (No 16985) for £563.50 from W Lamb, a credit customer in full settlement of invoice 23700
19th June	Paid rent of £400 with cheque 2402.
26th June	Paid wages of £2,798.56 by BACS
30th June	Paid rates £500 with cheque 2403
30th June	Received cheque (No 53486) for £310.00 from G Scott, a credit customer, in full settlement of invoice 23701

Show the entries in the cash book on the following page. The cash book had an opening debit balance of £2,856.29.

CASH BOOK

Date	Detail	Bank £		Date	Detail	Bank £	

13.2

The following is your bank statement for June 2015

IMMINGHAM BANK plc
14 Springfield Road, Brigg, DN20 3GF

STATEMENT

Account name:	Dawson Supplies	Statement no:	142

Account number :   12560798   30-25-81

Date	Details	Payments £	Receipts £	Balance £
2015				
1st June	Balance brought forward			3,056.29
1st June	CC		587.50	3,643.79
3rd June	Chq 2397	200.00		3,443.79
11th June	Chq 2399	30.00		3,413.79
12th June	Chq 2400	174.32		3,239.47
12th June	CC		528.72	3,768.19
15th June	Chq 2398	253.60		3,514.59
15th June	CC		622.29	4,136.88
16th June	DD Pei Hire Company	50.00		4,086.88
19th June	Chq 2401	172.50		3,914.38
25th June	BACS M D Sully		135.50	4,049.88
26th June	Chq 2402	400.00		3,649.88
30th June	BACS payment	2798.56		851.32
30th June	Bank Charges	13.50		837.82

CC:	Cash and cheques	DD:	Direct Debit
CT:	Credit transfer	O/D:	Overdrawn

Update the cash book with items in the statement not shown in the cash book. Total the columns and bring down a balance as at 1st July 2015

13.3

Prepare a bank reconciliation statement for the cash book prepared in task 13.1 and the bank statement in task 13.2

Bank Reconciliation Statement
31 May 2015

	£	£
Balance as per bank statement		
Less: unpresented cheques		
		———
Add: outstanding lodgements		
		———
Balance as per cash book		

Chapter 14

Journals and the Trial Balance

14.1

N Trent started a business on 1st June 2015 with the following:

- Opens a business bank account with £6,500 of her own money.

- She brings her own vehicle into full use of the business. The vehicle is worth £4,000.

- She brings £200 cash of her own money into the business as a till float.

- She will use her own computer as the business computer (shown in the Office Equipment account). It is worth £350.

- She introduces £500 worth of stock from her own collection.

You are to draw up her opening journal. You should clearly show her capital.

Date	Details	Dr	Cr

14.2

You work as an accounts assistant which sells decorating materials to the trade. Your supervisor has asked you to reconcile the sales ledger control account with the total of the subsidiary sales ledger.

A summary of the transactions with credit customers in June 2015 is as follows:

Balance of debtors on 1st June 2015	£57,001
Credit sales	£96,478
Payments received from credit customers	£102,523
Discounts allowed	£2,055
Sales returns	£5,250

The balances on the individual customer accounts in the sales ledger on 30th June 2015 are as follows:

W Blake	£8,295
J Constable	£10,428
T Gainsborough	£6,220
F Hals	£3,555
H Holbein	£9,269
W Turner	£3,275

(a)   Prepare a Sales Ledger Control Account for June 2015. Balance the account and bring down a balance as at 1st July 2015.

Dr	Sales Ledger Control Account				Cr
Date	Details	£	Date	Details	£

(b) Reconcile the sales ledger control account with the total of the subsidiary ledger accounts

```
┌─────────────────────────────────────────────────────────────────────────┐
│           Reconciliation of Sales Ledger Control Account                  │
│                         30ᵗʰ June 2015                                    │
│                                           £              £                │
│  _____                                                      │
│                                                                           │
│  _____                                                      │
│                                                                           │
│  _____                                                      │
│                                                                           │
│  _____                                                      │
│                                                                           │
│  _____                                                      │
│                                                                           │
│  _____                                     ____             │
│                                                                           │
│  TOTAL                                                                    │
│                                                                           │
│  TOTAL PER SALES LEDGER CONTROL                                           │
│                                                                           │
│  Discrepancy (if any)                                    ____             │
└─────────────────────────────────────────────────────────────────────────┘
```

(c) You are told that during the month a credit customer (J Pollock) has gone into liquidation. The amount owing was £2609. It has already been written off in the individual customer account but not yet in the main ledger. If necessary you are to prepare a journal to write this amount off. The date is 30ᵗʰ June 2015. (Ignore any VAT implications)

Date	Details	Dr	Cr
		£	£

14.3

You have the following list of balances taken from the accounting records on 30th June 2015.

Sales	£113,820
Sales Returns	£2,334
Debtors (SLC)	£6,669
Purchases	£63,000
Purchases Returns	£1,850
Creditors (PLC)	£5,656
Stock	£8,175
Office Equipment	£28,875
Company vehicles	£20,000
Bank Loan	£5,000
Cash	£892
Bank	£2,215 (credit balance)
VAT	£864 (credit balance)
Wages expense	£20,680
General expenses	£21,713
Drawings	£20,000
Capital	£63,000

You are to prepare a Trial Balance as at 30th June 2015. If it doesn't balance you are to raise a suspense account.

Trial Balance
30th June 2015

	Dr £	Cr £
Name of account		
Sales		
Sales Returns		
Purchases		
Purchase Returns		
Sales Ledger Control		
Purchases Ledger Control		
Office Equipment		
Vehicles		
Stock		
Cash		
Wages		
General expenses		
Bank		
Bank Loan		
VAT		
Drawings		
Capital		
Suspense		

14.4

Later the following errors and omissions are found:

a) A Sales invoice for £576.00 (including VAT) has been omitted completely from the accounts

b) A cheque for £805.00 from a debtor has not been recorded in the accounts

c) The cash book shows a cheque payment of £120.00 but no other entry has been made. It turns out that this is for the road fund license for one of the vehicles (which should be shown in the General Expenses account).

d) A sales invoice for £624.00 (including VAT) has been entered twice in the sales day book.

e) A cheque to a credit supplier has been recorded as £267.00 in the cash book but as £287.00 in the Purchases Ledger Control. The cheque is actually for £287.00

f) The owner of the business has taken £200 worth of goods for her own use, but this has not been recorded in the accounts.

g) Bank charges of £33.00 have been shown in the general expenses account, but the cash book has not been updated with this amount yet.

Make the journal entries to correct these errors (the date is 30th June 2015)

Date	Details	Dr £	Cr £

Date	Details	Dr £	Cr £

Date	Details	Dr £	Cr £

Date	Details	Dr £	Cr £

Date	Details	Dr	Cr
		£	£

Date	Details	Dr	Cr
		£	£

Date	Details	Dr	Cr
		£	£

Show the suspense account after the errors have been corrected. Balance the suspense account.

Dr			Suspense Account		Cr
Date	Details	£	Date	Details	£

14.5

Show the Trial Balance after the corrections have been made

Trial Balance (Amended)
30th June 2015

	Dr £	Cr £
Name of account		
Sales		
Sales Returns		
Purchases		
Purchase Returns		
Sales Ledger Control		
Purchases Ledger Control		
Office Equipment		
Vehicles		
Stock		
Cash		
Wages		
General expenses		
Bank		
Bank Loan		
VAT		
Drawings		
Capital		
Suspense		

14.6

You work at a garden centre. The following transactions took place on 30th June 2015

SALES DAY BOOK									SDB 105	
Date	Invoice	Customer	Total		Sales		VAT			
			£	p	£	p	£	p		
2015										
30th June	23986	L C Brown	720	00	600	00	120	00		
30th June	23987	P Thrower	480	00	400	00	80	00		
30th June	23988	A Titchmarsh	1200	00	1000	00	200	00		
30th June	23989	C Dimmock	624	00	520	00	104	00		
		TOTAL FOR THE DAY	3024	00	2520	00	504	00		

SALES RETURNS DAY BOOK									SRDB 15	
Date	Invoice	Customer	Total		Sales		VAT			
			£	p	£	p	£	p		
2015										
30th June	CN 47	A Titchmarsh	48	00	40	00	8	00		
30th June	CN 48	P Thrower	192	00	160	00	32	00		
		TOTAL FOR THE DAY	240	00	200	00	40	00		

CASH BOOK

Date	Detail	Discounts Allowed		Bank		Date	Detail	Discounts Received		Bank	
2015		£		£		2015		£		£	
30/06	L C Brown	75	00	3450	00	30/06	Balance b/d			577	00
30/06	P Thrower			750	00	30/06	Wages			3200	00
						30/06	Balance c/d			423	00
		75	00	4200	00					4200	00

You have the following relevant accounts at the start of the day:

Credit customers

L C Brown   £6,749
P Thrower   £1,628
A Titchmarsh £5,796
C Dimmock   £2,150
J Loudon   £336

Sales Ledger Control	£16,659
Sales	£180,754
Sales Returns	£1,748
Discounts allowed	£405
Office expenses	£1,680
Wages	£32,232
VAT (credit balance)	£1470
Bad debts written off	£208
Suspense account	£96 (debit)

You are told that:

- J Loudon has gone into liquidation and his account needs to be written off. VAT relief is available on the debt.

- Office expenses of £40 + VAT was credited to the expense account and the VAT account in error. (It was recorded correctly in the cash book).

- The payment of the window cleaning bill for £120 (no VAT) was debited to the wages account rather than the office expenses account in error.

You are to record the transactions from the day book and the cash book in the following accounts having first entered the opening balances. Show the journals for the adjustments above and then enter them in the accounts. Balance the accounts.

SALES LEDGER

Dr			L C Brown Account		Cr
Date	Details	£	Date	Details	£

Dr			P Thrower Account		Cr
Date	Details	£	Date	Details	£

Dr			A Titchmarsh Account		Cr
Date	Details	£	Date	Details	£

Dr			C Dimmock Account		Cr
Date	Details	£	Date	Details	£

Dr			J Loudon Account		Cr
Date	Details	£	Date	Details	£

MAIN LEDGER

Dr			Sales Account		Cr
Date	Details	£	Date	Details	£

Dr			Sales Ledger Control Account		Cr
Date	Details	£	Date	Details	£

Dr			Sales Returns Account		Cr
Date	Details	£	Date	Details	£

Dr			Discounts Allowed Account		Cr
Date	Details	£	Date	Details	£

Dr			Office Expenses Account		Cr
Date	Details	£	Date	Details	£

Dr			Wages Expense Account		Cr
Date	Details	£	Date	Details	£

Dr	VAT Account				Cr
Date	Details	£	Date	Details	£

Dr	Bad Debts Account				Cr
Date	Details	£	Date	Details	£

Dr	Suspense Account				Cr
Date	Details	£	Date	Details	£

Date	Details	Dr	Cr
		£	£

Date	Details	Dr	Cr
		£	£

Date	Details	Dr	Cr
		£	£

14.7

In addition to those accounts shown above you have the following balances:

Premises	£250,000
Motor Vehicles	£30,000
Office Equipment	£10,460
Motor expenses	£1,050
Stock	£7,487
Cash	£250
Drawings	£25,042
Capital	£283,000
Heat & Light	£2,526
Rates	£3,860
Purchases Ledger Control	£6,559
Purchases	£97,686
Purchases Returns	£1,551
Discounts Received	£377
Rent Received	£7,500
Bank charges	£399

Transfer the balances calculated in 4.6, from the cash book, and from the balances above to the trial balance shown on the next page.

Trial Balance
30th June 2015

	Dr £	Cr £
Name of account		
Premises		
Motor vehicles		
Office Equipment		
Stock		
Bank		
Cash		
Sales Ledger Control		
Purchases Ledger Control		
VAT		
Drawings		
Capital		
Sales		
Sales Returns		
Discounts Allowed		
Purchases		
Purchases Returns		
Discounts Received		
Rent Received		
Wages		
Office Expenses		
Motor Expenses		
Heat & Light		
Bad Debts		
Rates		
Bank charges		
Suspense		

14.8

The accounting records showed the following balances at the end of the year:

Capital (money invested by the owner in the business)	£316,000
Business premises	£300,000
Bank overdraft	£30,000
Delivery vehicles	£20,000
Computers used in the offices	£10,000
Stock of goods	£6,000
Creditors (amounts owed by the business)	£15,000
Debtors (amounts owed to the business)	£25,000

a) Sort the accounts into:

- Assets
- Liabilities
- Capital

b) Insert the figures into the accounting equation and ensure it balances.

c) The bank overdraft is increased to buy more stock costing £2,000. Adjust the totals in the accounting equation and make sure it still balances.

PRACTICE EXAMINATION

1

MARTIN'S MOBILES

PRACTICE EXAMINATION 1
Martin's Mobiles

This exam paper is in TWO sections.

You must show competence in BOTH sections. So, try to complete EVERY task in BOTH sections.

Section 1 contains 10 tasks and Section 2 contains 20 tasks.

You should spend about 75 minutes on Section 1 and 105 minutes on Section 2.

You should include all essential calculations in your answers.

Both sections are based on the business described below.

Introduction

- Martin Butler is the owner of Martin's Mobiles, a business which supplies mobile phones.

- You are employed by the business as a bookkeeper.

- The business uses a manual accounting system.

- Double entry takes place in the main (general) ledger. Individual accounts of debtors and creditors are kept in subsidiary ledgers as memorandum accounts.

- Payments and receipts from the bank current account are recorded in the cash-book, which is part of the double entry system.

- The VAT rate is 20%.

- Assume today's date is 31st July 2015 unless you are told otherwise.

Section 1 – Double entry bookkeeping and trial balance

You should spend about 75 minutes on this section.

Note
Show your answers with a tick, words or figures, as appropriate.

Task 1.1

The following sales invoices are ready for entry in the sales day book.

Invoice 2786 to Capital Communications	for	£1,800 plus VAT
Invoice 2787 to Mobile Mania	for	£840 plus VAT
Invoice 2788 to The Mobile Box	for	£3,600 plus VAT
Invoice 2789 to Keep Talking	for	£1,560 plus VAT

Enter these invoices into the sales day book below and total each column.

Date 2015	Details	Invoice number	Total £	VAT £	Net £
31 July					
31 July					
31 July					
31 July					
Total					

85

Task 1.2

Refer to the sales day book entries you made in task 1.1.

(a)   **What will be the entries in the subsidiary (sales) ledger?**

Subsidiary (sales) ledger

Account name	Amount £	Debit ✓	Credit ✓

(b)   **What will be the entries in the main ledger?**

Main ledger

Account name	Amount £	Debit ✓	Credit ✓

Task 1.3

The following purchases invoices have been entered in the purchases day book as shown below.

Date 2015	Details	Invoice number	Total £	VAT £	Net £
31 July	Digiphones	23968	5,280	880	4,400
31 July	The Phone Shed	PS2340	768	128	640
31 July	Happy Talk Phones	3605	7,728	1,288	6,440
31 July	Foanz Place	66579	2,016	336	1,680
Total			15,792	2,632	13,160

What will be the entries in the main ledger?

Main ledger

Account name	Amount £	Debit ✓	Credit ✓

Task 1.4

On 31st July a credit note for £3,760 plus VAT was received from a supplier

What will be the entries in the main ledger?

Main ledger

Account name	Amount £	Debit ✓	Credit ✓

Task 1.5

On 31st July Martin's Mobiles sold goods for £1,760 plus VAT, for cash, to a customer who did not have a credit account.

What will be the entries in the main ledger?

Main ledger

Account name	Amount £	Debit ✓	Credit ✓

Task 1.6

The following transactions took place on 31st July 2015 and have been entered into the receipts side of the cash book as shown below. No entries have yet been made in the ledgers.

Date 2015	Details	Discount allowed £	Bank £
31 July	The Mobile Box (credit customer)	317	14,582
31 July	Keep Talking (credit customer)		3,290

(a)   What will be the entries in the subsidiary (sales) ledger?

Subsidiary (sales) ledger

Account name	Amount £	Debit ✓	Credit ✓

(b)   What will be the entries in the main ledger?

Main ledger

Account name	Amount £	Debit ✓	Credit ✓

Task 1.7

(a)   **Record the following details in the office expenses account below.**

1st July	Balance b/d (debit)	£1,650
15th July	Bank payment	£1,965
31st July	Journal (Credit)	£80

(b)   **Total the account showing clearly the balance carried down at 31st July and the balance brought down at 1st August.**

Office expenses

Date 2015	Details	Amount £	Date 2013	Details	Amount £

Task 1.8

Martin's Mobiles buys from, and sells to, Bells Phones Company. It has been agreed that balances owing and owed should be offset against each other.

What will be the entries in the main ledger to record a contra entry of £1,250?

Main ledger

Account name	Amount £	Debit ✓	Credit ✓

90

Task 1.9

Record the journal entries needed in the main ledger to deal with the information below. You do not need to show dates and narratives

(a)   £300 has been debited to the discounts received account instead of credited.

Account name	Amount £	Debit ✓	Credit ✓
Suspense account			
Discounts received			
Suspense account			
Discounts received			

(b)   A payment of £350 for motor repairs has been debited to the motor vehicles account instead of the motor expenses account.

Account name	Amount £	Debit ✓	Credit ✓
Motor expenses			
Motor vehicles			

(c)   A credit customer, A Daley Ltd, has gone into liquidation, owing Martin's Mobiles £1,880 plus VAT. The net amount and the VAT must be written off in the main ledger.

Account name	Amount £	Debit ✓	Credit ✓

Task 1.10

Below is a list of balances to be transferred to the trial balance as at 31st July.

Place the figures in the debit or credit column, as appropriate, and total each column.

Account name	Amount £	Debit £	Credit £
Premises	200,000		
Motor Vehicles	15,000		
Office Equipment	7.600		
Stock	7,460		
Bank (debit balance)	2.579		
Sales Ledger Control	19,645		
Purchases Ledger Control	18,790		
VAT (credit balance)	674		
Drawings	15,250		
Capital	196,000		
Sales	143,395		
Sales Returns	685		
Discounts Allowed	114		
Purchases	89,535		
Purchases Returns	1,495		
Discounts Received	185		
Rent Received	2,500		
Wages & Salaries	4,425		
Office expenses	524		
Petty Cash	250		
Miscellaneous expenses	63		
Suspense account (credit balance)	91		
TOTALS			

Section 2 – Tasks and questions

You should spend about 105 minutes on this section.

Notes

- You do not need to adjust any accounts in Section 1 as part of any of the following tasks
- Show your answers with a tick, words or figures, as appropriate.

Task 2.1

You pay your suppliers by BACS. The Phone Shed is offering a discount if it receives payment by Friday 31st July 2015.

(a) **By what date should you instruct your bank to pay this amount in order for it to reach The Phone Shed by this date?**

_____

(b) **Give ONE advantage of paying in this way.**

_____

_____

(c) **Will Martin's Mobiles be shown as a debtor or creditor in The Phone Shed's accounts?**

Debtor   /   Creditor

Task 2.2

Martin's Mobiles has just opened a new credit account for a new customer, Ultimate Phones, which brings the total number of customers to 30.

(a) **Suggest an appropriate four-character alpha-numeric ledger code for this account.**

(b) **In which ledger would you expect to see this account?**

	✓
Main ledger	
Subsidiary Sales ledger	
Subsidiary Purchases ledger	

Task 2.3

The petty cash book has been partially completed for July, as shown below.

Date 2015	Details	Amount £	Date 2015	Details	Total £	Stationery £	Postage £	Travel £
1 July	Balance b/f	100	10 July	Postage Stamps	36			
			17 July	Pens	10			
			24 July	Taxi fare	7			
			31 July	Envelopes	12			
	Total			Total				

(a) Complete the analysis columns for the items purchased from petty cash (ignore VAT).

(b) Total and balance the account. Showing clearly the balance carried down at 31 July.

(c) Enter the balance brought down at 1 August, showing clearly he date, details, and amount. You do NOT need to restore the imprest amount.

(d) What amount will be required to restore the imprest level to £100?

Task 2.4

During July there was a random check of the cash in the petty cash box against the balance shown in the petty cash book. There was £47 in cash but the balance in the petty cash book was £54.

Suggest THREE possible reasons for this discrepancy

1	
2	
3	

Task 2.5

During the last VAT quarter sales were £51,385 **plus VAT**. Purchases totalled £37,698 **including VAT**.

(a)   What was the amount of VAT payable on sales made?

(b)   What was the amount of VAT included in the purchases figure?

(c)   What would have been the balance on the VAT account at the end of the quarter?

(d)   Is the amount calculated in (c) above payable to HM Revenue & Customs or receivable from them?

Task 2.6

Martin's Mobiles is considering buying a new delivery vehicle. Your supervisor is wondering whether he could ask the bank for an overdraft.

(a)   What is an overdraft?

_____

_____

_____

(b)   Would the overdraft show in the trial balance at Martin's mobiles as a debit or a credit balance?

Debit   /   Credit

Task 2.7

What document would you send or receive in the following circumstances?

		✓
To accompany a cheque to your supplier	Receipt	
	Delivery Note	
	Remittance Advice	

		✓
To advise the customer of amounts outstanding and already paid	Statement	
	Delivery Note	
	Invoice	

		✓
To advise a customer that an order has been received and when the goods will be sent	Receipt	
	Advice note	
	Remittance Advice	

Task 2.8

Complete the following sentences by inserting the relevant legal terms

(a)   A price shown on the supermarket shelf is called _____

_____

(b)   For a contract to exist there must be an intention to create legal relations, an

agreement, and a _____

(c)   A contract is said to be discharged through agreement, frustration, breach of

contract or _____

Task 2.9

The following is a summary of the wage due an employee during July together with
deductions.

I Livingston			
Gross Wage	£1,960	Tax	£279
Employee's NIC	£114	Employer's NIC	£183
Employee's pension contr.	£100	Employer's pension contr.	£100

(a)   Calculate the net wage

(b)   What amount is payable to HM Revenue & Customs?

(c)   What is the total expense to the company?

98

Task 2.10

Would each of the following be a debit or credit entry in the Wages and Salaries control account in the Main ledger?

Account name	Debit ✓	Credit ✓
Net wages paid to employees		
Employee's pension contribution		
Employee's NIC		
Gross Wages		

Task 2.11

Apart from invoices charged to the customer name THREE other items which may be found on a statement of account.

1	
2	
3	

Task 2.12

Martin's Mobile customers can pay by debit card or credit card if they wish to purchase a phone over the internet or by phone.

(a) **Briefly explain the difference between a debit card and a credit card.**

_____

_____

_____

(b) **Name THREE credit card details the customer will be asked for when payment is taken over the phone.**

1	
2	
3	

Task 2.13

Martin's Mobiles has received the following cheque from a customer.

IMMINGHAM BANK plc		30 - 25 - 81
14 Springfield Road, Brigg, DN20 3GF		

Date _27ᵗʰ August 2013_

Pay   _Martin's Mobiles_

One Hundred and Fifty   A/C Payee   _Pounds_   £ | _100.00_

only

Cheque number   Sort Code   Account number
500013   30-25-81   12560798

R Obermann

(a)   Give THREE reasons why the cheque cannot be paid by Immingham Bank

1	
2	
3	

(b)   What does the 'A/C Payee' crossing mean?

_____

_____

_____

(c)   If the date were missing from the cheque altogether could Martin's Mobiles fill this in themselves?

Yes / No

Task 2.14

Martin's Mobiles is considering offering discounts customers to boost trade.

What is the name of the discount for:

	Settlement Discount ✓	Bulk Discount ✓	Trade Discount ✓
A 10% discount for orders over £1,000			
A 3% discount for payment within 10 days			
A 15% discount to other mobile phone traders			

Task 2.15

When customers pay cash, the money is kept in the till until Friday afternoon when your supervisor takes it to the bank on his way home. He quickly counts the money before he leaves for the bank. There is often more than £1,000 to bank.

Suggest THREE changes that could be made to improve security

1
2
3

Task 2.16

Martin's Mobiles' transactions in July included the items listed below.

State whether each is a capital transaction or a revenue transaction

Transaction	Capital or Revenue
Annual decoration of office	
Purchase of a new computer	
Repair of broken window	
Wages paid to employees	

Task 2.17

This is a summary of transactions with customers during July

(a) **Show whether each entry will be a debit or credit in the Sales ledger control account in the Main Ledger.**

Account name	Amount £	Debit ✓	Credit ✓
Balance of debtors at 1st July 2015	18,129		
Goods sold on credit (inclusive of VAT)	7,656		
Money received from credit customers	6,085		
Discounts allowed	35		
Goods returned by credit customers (inclusive of VAT)	20		

(b) **What will be the balance brought down on 1st August on the above account?** ✓

Dr £19,645	
Cr £19,645	
Dr £19,575	
Cr £19,575	
Dr £16,613	
Cr £16,613	

Task 2.17, continued

The following opening balances were in the subsidiary sales ledger on 1 August:

Capital Communications   £4,744 debit
Eezee Phone   £346 credit
Keep Talking   £3,824 debit
Mobile Mania   £987 debit
The Mobile Box   £9,744 debit

(c) **Reconcile the balances shown above with the sales ledger control account balance you have calculated in part (b)**

	£
Sales ledger control account balance as at 1 August	
Total of subsidiary sales ledger accounts as at 1 August	
Difference	

The sales ledger control account and the subsidiary sales ledger do not agree.

(d) **What may have caused the difference?**

_____

_____

_____

_____

Data

On 27 July Martin's Mobiles received the following bank statement as at 24 July

---

LINDUM BANK plc
Main Road, Lincoln, LN2 3RQ

STATEMENT

Account name: Martin's Mobiles Statement no: 97

Account number : 23975618 09-26-54

Date	Details	Payments £	Receipts £	Balance £
2015				
1st July	Balance brought forward			1,933
5th July	Chq 001481	200		1,733
10th July	Chq 001484	2,450		717 O/D
12th July	Chq 001485	199		916 O/D
15th July	Chq 001487	250		1,166 O/D
17th July	CT The Mobile Box		4,750	3,584
19th July	Chq 001489	75		3,509
22nd July	DD Happy Talk Phones	1,560		1,949
23rd July	DD The Phone Shed	175		1,774
24th July	CT Keep Talking		1,750	3,524
24th July	Bank Charges	37		3,487
24th July	Interest received		5	3,492

CC:	Cash and cheques	DD:	Direct Debit
CT:	Credit transfer	O/D:	Overdrawn

The cash book as at 24 July is shown below

Date 2015	Details	Bank £	Date 2015	Cheque Number	Details	Bank £
01 July	Balance b/f	1,733	5 July	001484	Digiphones	2,450
10 July	Eezee Phone	1,250	8 July	001485	NGJ Ltd	199
15 July	Mobile Mania	1,500	8 July	001486	P Erskine	88
			11 July	001487	T Alexander Ltd	250
			15 July	001488	A Sarin	126
			15 July	001489	E Richards	75
			22 July		Happy Talk Phones	1,560

Task 2.18

(a)   Check the items on the bank statement against the items in the cash book
(b)   Update the cash book as needed
(c)   Total the cash book and clearly show the balance carried down at 24th July (closing balance) AND brought down at 25th July (opening balance)

Note:
You do not need to adjust the accounts in Section 1.

Task 2.18, continued

(d) **Prepare a bank reconciliation statement as at 24 July.**

Note:
Do not make any entries in the shaded boxes

Bank reconciliation statement as at 24 July 2015	
Balance per bank statement	£
Add:	
Name:	£
Name:	£
Total to add	£
Less:	
Name:	£
Name:	£
Total to subtract	£
Balance as per cash book	£

Task 2.19

On 1 August Martin's Mobiles received the following cash and cheque

Cash   **Cheque**

4 x £10 notes   1 x £4,680
6 x £5 notes
13 x £2 coins
12 x £1 coins
7 x 50p coins

Complete the following paying in slip

Date 01 August 2015	Lindum Bank plc Lincoln	£50 notes	
		£20 notes	
		£10 notes	
	Account Martin's Mobiles	£5 notes	
		£2 coin	
		£1 coin	
	Paid in by *Martin Butler*	Other coin	
		Total cash	
		Cheques, POs	
	09-26-54 23975618	Total £	

109

Task 2.20

Martin Butler is concerned that the account of Capital Communications is overdue for payment. A letter had already been sent in June, but there has been no response from Capital Communications.

Using the letterhead below, draft a letter to W Cooke at Capital Communications, ready for Martin's signature.

- **Include that there has been a previous reminder**
- **State that there is a balance outstanding of £4,744**
- **Explain that the debt relates to invoice number 3567 of 24 April 2015**
- **Request a payment by return or legal action will be taken**
- **State that a copy of the invoice is enclosed**

MARTIN'S
MOBILES

225 Park Road,
Lincoln,
LN6 3WD

Mr W Cooke
Capital Communications
Kilburn High Road,
London,
NW2 3RT

PRACTICE EXAMINATION

2

DAVE'S DIGITAL

PRACTICE EXAMINATION
Dave's Digital

This exam paper is in TWO sections.

You must show competence in BOTH sections. So, try to complete EVERY task in BOTH sections.

Section 1 contains 10 tasks and Section 2 contains 20 tasks.

You should spend about 75 minutes on Section 1 and 105 minutes on Section 2.

You should include all essential calculations in your answers.

Both sections are based on the business described below.

Introduction

- David Rouse is the owner of Dave's Digital, a business which specialises in digital TVs and TV accessories.

- You are employed by the business as a bookkeeper.

- The business uses a manual accounting system.

- Double entry takes place in the main (general) ledger. Individual accounts of debtors and creditors are kept in subsidiary ledgers as memorandum accounts.

- Payments and receipts from the bank current account are recorded in the cash-book, which is part of the double entry system.

- The VAT rate is 20%.

- Assume today's date is 31st August 2015 unless you are told otherwise.

Section 1 – Double entry bookkeeping and trial balance

You should spend about 75 minutes on this section.

Note
Show your answers with a tick, words or figures, as appropriate.

Task 1.1

The following transactions all took place on 31st August and have been entered into the purchases day book as shown below. No entries have been made in the ledger.

Date 2015	Details	Invoice number	Total £	VAT £	Net £
31 August	Clearvision Ltd	S1954	6,240	1,040	5,200
31 August	Telemagic plc	3657	1,440	240	1,200
31 August	Sound & Vision Ltd	SV1169	816	136	680
31 August	Tipachi plc	59876	2,400	400	2,000
Total			**10,896**	**1,816**	**9,080**

(a)   What will be the entries in the subsidiary (purchases) ledger?

Subsidiary (purchases) ledger

Account name	Amount £	Debit ✓	Credit ✓

Task 1.1, continued

(b)   **What will be the entries in the main ledger?**

Main ledger

Account name	Amount £	Debit ✓	Credit ✓

Task 1.2

Sales invoices have been prepared and partially entered in the sales day book as shown below.

(a)   **Complete the entries in the sales day book by inserting the VAT and the net amounts for each invoice.**

(b)   **Total the last three columns of the sales day book**

Date 2015	Details	Invoice number	Total £	VAT £	Net £
31 August	Tony's TVs	5369	3,360		
31 August	TVs 4 U	5370	768		
31 August	Switched On	5371	10,224		
31 August	Total Entertainment	5372	864		
Total					

Task 1.3

Refer to the sales day book in Task 1.2

(a)   **What will be the entries in the subsidiary (sales) ledger?**

Subsidiary (sales) ledger

Account name	Amount £	Debit ✓	Credit ✓

(b)   **What will be the entries in the main ledger?**

Main ledger

Account name	Amount £	Debit ✓	Credit ✓

Task 1.4

The following transactions all took place on 31st August and have been entered into the purchases returns day book as shown below. No entries have been made in the ledger.

Date 2015	Details	Credit Note number	Total £	VAT £	Net £
31 August	Clearvision Ltd	SC54	96	16	80
31 August	Tipachi plc	CN29	240	40	200
Total			336	56	280

(a)   **What will be the entries in the subsidiary (purchases) ledger?**

Subsidiary (purchases) ledger

Account name	Amount £	Debit ✓	Credit ✓

(b)   **What will be the entries in the main ledger?**

Main ledger

Account name	Amount £	Debit ✓	Credit ✓

Task 1.5

On 31st August a customer bought goods to a value of £1,880 plus VAT for cash.

What will be the entries in the main ledger?

Main ledger

Account name	Amount £	Debit ✓	Credit ✓

Task 1.6

The following transactions all took place on 31 August and have been entered in the cash book as shown below. No entries have yet been made in the ledgers.

Date 2015	Details	Discount Allowed £	Bank £	Date 2015	Details	VAT £	Bank £
31 Aug	Balance b/f		6,570	31 Aug	Office Equipment	170	1,170
31 Aug	Switched On	138	3,563	31 Aug	Rent		825
31 Aug	VAT refund		197	31 Aug	Telephone	21	141
				31 Aug	Petty Cash		150
				31 Aug	Tipachi plc (creditor)		1,260
				31 Aug	Balance c/d		6,784
		138	10,330			191	10,330
1 Sept	Balance b/d		6,784				

117

Task 1.6, continued

What will be the entries to record these payments in the Subsidiary sales ledger, the Subsidiary purchases ledger, and the Main ledger?

Subsidiary (sales) ledger

Account name	Amount £	Debit ✓	Credit ✓

Subsidiary (purchases) ledger

Account name	Amount £	Debit ✓	Credit ✓

Main ledger

Account name	Amount £	Debit ✓	Credit ✓

Task 1.7

(a) Record the following details in the petty cash control account below.

1st August   Balance b/d (debit)   £200
31st August   Total payments from petty cash book for month   £150
31st August   Top up from bank   £150

(b) Total the account showing clearly the balance carried down at 31st August and the balance brought down at 1st September.

Petty Cash Control

Date 2015	Details	Amount £	Date 2015	Details	Amount £

Task 1.8

Record the journal entries needed in the Main Ledger to deal with the following items.

Note:
You do not need to give narratives. You may not need to use all the lines.

(a) An amount of £75 has been debited to the miscellaneous expenses account instead of the motor expenses account.

Account name	Amount £	Debit ✓	Credit ✓

Task 1.8, continued

(b) Purchases returns of £200 have been entered as £2,000 in the Main ledger accounts (ignore VAT)

Account name	Amount £	Debit ✓	Credit ✓

(c) A credit customer, JD's Ltd, has ceased trading. It owes Dave's Digital £1,760 plus VAT. The net amount and the VAT must be written off in the Main Ledger.

Account name	Amount £	Debit ✓	Credit ✓

Task 1.9

During the month a trial balance was extracted which did not balance and an amount of £123 was credited to the suspense account. The following two errors have now been discovered.

1. An amount of £132 has been omitted from the discounts received account.

2. A payment of £254 has been recorded as £245 in the motor expenses account.

What entries are needed in the Main Ledger to correct these errors?

Account name	Amount £	Debit ✓	Credit ✓

121

Task 1.10

Below is a list of balances to be transferred to the trial balance as at 31st July.

Place the figures in the debit or credit column, as appropriate, and total each column.

Account name	Amount £	Debit £	Credit £
Motor Vehicles	16,212		
Office Equipment	17,572		
Stock	30,560		
Bank (debit balance)	6,784		
Petty cash control	200		
Sales Ledger Control	163,257		
Purchases Ledger Control	119,415		
VAT owing	22,719		
Capital	29,129		
Sales	611,974		
Sales Returns	458		
Discounts Allowed	336		
Discounts Received	372		
Purchases	472,160		
Purchases Returns	4,759		
Wages	69,372		
Travel expenses	2,946		
Motor expenses	1,572		
Office expenses	4,770		
Bad Debts	1,222		
Miscellaneous expenses	947		
TOTALS			

Section 2 – Tasks and questions

You should spend about 105 minutes on this section.

Notes
- You do not need to adjust any accounts in Section 1 as part of any of the following tasks
- Show your answers with a tick, words or figures, as appropriate.

Task 2.1

Dave's Digital operates a petty cash imprest system.

(a)   What is an imprest system?

_____

_____

_____

You counted the following notes and coins in the cash tin before the imprest was restored.

Notes and coins

1	x	£10
3	x	£5
5	x	£2
5	x	£1
7	x	50p
5	x	10p
10	x	5p
25	x	2p
50	x	1p

The balance on the petty cash control account was £50.00.

(b)   Complete the following reconciliation

Petty cash reconciliation	£	p
Balance on petty cash control account		
Cash in hand		
Difference		

Task 2.1, continued

(c) **Suggest THREE possible reasons for the difference**

1) _____

_____

2) _____

_____

3) _____

_____

Task 2.2

You have been asked to calculate the amount of VAT owing to HM Revenue & Customs for the last VAT quarter, All sales and all purchases are subject to VAT.

(a) **Complete the VAT calculation summary below.**

	VAT amount £
Sales £262,280 **excluding** VAT	
Purchases £237,726 **including** VAT	
VAT Payable	

(b) **What will be the accounting entries required to record payment of this amount by cheque?**

Account name	Debit ✓	Credit ✓

Task 2.3

Dave's Digitals has received the following invoice on 1 September 2013. You have been asked to pay this invoice immediately.

SOUND & VISION Ltd

127 South Street, Keighley, BD21 7RQ

Invoice

Number: SV1180

VAT Registration Number 312 6587 41

Invoice
to

| Dave's Digitals |
| 32 Park Street |
| South Shields |
| NE33 6TY |

Date/ tax point: 31st August 2015

Account:

Your reference: 7651

Product Code	Item	Quantity	Price £	Total £
	Satellite Dishes	10	40.00	400.00
Goods Total				400.00
Trade Discount @ 10%				40.00
Subtotal				360.00
VAT @ 20%				69.84
Invoice Total				**429.84**

Terms

3% settlement discount for settlement within 7 days, other wise 30 days net

---

Task 2.3, continued

(a)   What is the amount to be paid to Sound & Vision Ltd?

_____

(b)   What is the purpose of a TRADE discount?

	✓
To reward customers who pay in cash	
To offer a lower price to an organisation within the same trade	
To reduce the price of goods which are damaged	

(c)   To which customers might Dave's Digital offer a BULK discount?

	✓
Those placing large orders	
Those with many branches	
Those who have been customers for many years	

Task 2.4

What document would you send or receive in the following circumstances?

		✓
To adjust the customer's account for goods returned	Invoice	
	Credit Note	
	Remittance Advice	

		✓
To accompany and list the goods ordered	Statement	
	Delivery Note	
	Receipt	

		✓
To acknowledge payment for goods	Receipt	
	Advice note	
	Remittance Advice	

Task 2.5

The following errors have been made in the accounts of Dave's Digital.

Show whether the errors cause an imbalance by selecting the correct answer

(a)   Discount allowed has not been taken by a customer

	✓
The trial balance will balance	
The trial balance will not balance	

Task 2.5, continued

(b)   A purchase invoice has been entered correctly in the main ledger, but omitted from the subsidiary purchases ledger.

	✓
The trial balance will balance	
The trial balance will not balance	

(c)   A payment for service to a vehicle has been entered into the miscellaneous expenses instead of the motor expenses.

	✓
The trial balance will balance	
The trial balance will not balance	

(d)   A cash purchases has been entered into the cash book but not into the purchases account or the VAT account.

	✓
The trial balance will balance	
The trial balance will not balance	

(e)   VAT on a Sales invoice has been incorrectly calculated

	✓
The trial balance will balance	
The trial balance will not balance	

Task 2.6

Dave's Digital gives all stock items a code number when it arrives.

Explain why this is done.

_____

_____

_____

_____

Task 2.7

A cheque has been received by Dave's Digital dated 27th August 2014 and the bank will not accept it.

(a)   **Explain why.**

_____

_____

_____

(b)   **If a cheque was paid into the bank on Monday morning, when can you be certain a withdrawal be made against that cheque?**

_____

_____

Task 2.8

On 1 August Dave's Digital offered to supply some goods to a customer. The customer posted the acceptance on 3 August and it was received at Dave's Digital on 6 August.

What is the date on which the contract was formed?

	✓
1 August	
3 August	
6 August	

Task 2.9

Which TWO items would you expect to see in a Wages and Salaries control account?

	✓
Gross wages paid to employees	
Drawings by the owner of the business	
Payment to 'Office Clean Ltd' for cleaning the office	
Payment by the employee to a trade union	
Payment to creditors	

Task 2.10

Dave's Digital's transactions in August included the items listed below.

State whether each is a capital transaction or a revenue transaction

Transaction	Capital or Revenue
Replacement of a worn tyre on a delivery vehicle	
Purchase goods for resale	
Purchase of new vehicle	
12 months' road fund licence for the new vehicle	

Task 2.11

Dave's Digital makes use of the BACS system for making payments.

Which TWO payment types would you recommend for processing using BACS?

	✓
Payment of wages to permanent staff	
Top-up of the petty cash	
Payment for fuel for the delivery vans	
Payment to creditors	

Task 2.12

The Sale of Goods Act sets out what a customer is entitled to expect when buying goods from a shop.

Which one of the following is NOT one of the conditions set out in the Sale of Goods Act?

	✓
Goods must be of 'satisfactory quality'	
Goods must be of 'fit for purpose'	
Goods must represent 'value for money'	
Goods must be 'as described'	

Task 2.13

Dave's Digital often receives payment by cheque in the post.

(a)   List THREE checks the cashier should make when receiving the cheque.

1) _____

_____

2) _____

_____

3) _____

_____

Task 2.13, continued

(b) **On a cheque what is:**

    i)   **The payee**

_____

_____

    ii)   **The drawer**

_____

_____

    iii)   **The drawee**

_____

_____

(c) **State THREE other methods of payment customers are likely to use without visiting the shop**

1	
2	
3	

Task 2.14

David Rouse has agreed to buy a new car for business use. The seller does not want to accept a business cheque and does not want cash.

(a)   What service is offered by banks would you recommend?

_____

(b)   What will be the accounting entries required in the Main Ledger to record this purchase? (Ignore VAT)

Account name	Debit ✓	Credit ✓

Task 2.15

Name TWO source documents from which a sales invoice might be prepared

1	
2	

Task 2.16

Dave's digitals usually places orders for goods by posting them to its suppliers.

Suggest THREE alternative ways of placing orders for goods

1	
2	
3	

Task 2.17

Dave's Digital had the following information relating to purchases for August.

1st August	Credit balance brought down	£111,022
31st August	Credit purchases for the month	£67,451
	Purchases returns	£679
	Payments made to creditors	£57,279
	Transfer of a credit balance to the sales ledger	£1,100

(a) **Complete the purchases ledger control account from the above information.**

(b) **Total the account showing clearly the balance carried down at 31st August and the balance brought down at 1st September.**

Purchases Ledger Control

Date 2015	Details	Amount £	Date 2015	Details	Amount £

Task 2.17, continued

The following balances were in the subsidiary purchases ledger on 1st September.

Clearvision Ltd	£30,454
Shibota plc	£20,375
Sound & Vision Ltd	£14,889
Telemagic plc	£37,629
Tipachi plc	£16,086

(c) **Reconcile the balances shown above with the purchse ledger control account balance you have calculated in part (b)**

	£
Purchase ledger control account balance as at 1 September	
Total of subsidiary purchases ledger accounts as at 1 September	
Difference	

The purchases ledger control and subsidiary purchases ledger do not agree.

(d) **Which ONE of the following errors might have caused the difference?**

	✔
One of the accounts in the subsidiary ledger has been understated	
One of the accounts in the subsidiary ledger has been overstated	
One supplier has offered a discount	
Dave's Digital has underpaid a supplier	
Dave's Digital has overpaid a supplier	

136

Data

On 24 August Martin's Mobiles received the following bank statement as at 21 August

<table>
<tr><td colspan="5" align="center">EBOR BANK plc
High Street, York, YO1 4TP</td></tr>
<tr><td colspan="5">STATEMENT</td></tr>
<tr><td>Account name:</td><td>Dave's Digital</td><td>Statement no:</td><td colspan="2" align="right">149</td></tr>
<tr><td>Account number :</td><td>12798564</td><td></td><td colspan="2">23-17-49</td></tr>
<tr>
<th>Date</th>
<th>Details</th>
<th>Payments
£</th>
<th>Receipts
£</th>
<th>Balance
£</th>
</tr>
<tr><td>2015</td><td></td><td></td><td></td><td></td></tr>
<tr><td>3rd Aug</td><td>Balance brought forward</td><td></td><td></td><td>13,135</td></tr>
<tr><td>7th Aug</td><td>Chq 237416</td><td>542</td><td></td><td>12,593</td></tr>
<tr><td>11th Aug</td><td>Chq 237417</td><td>6,974</td><td></td><td>5,619</td></tr>
<tr><td>11th Aug</td><td>Chq 237409</td><td>199</td><td></td><td>5,420</td></tr>
<tr><td>17th Aug</td><td>Chq 237418</td><td>377</td><td></td><td>5,043</td></tr>
<tr><td>17th Aug</td><td>CT TVs 4 U</td><td></td><td>960</td><td>6,003</td></tr>
<tr><td>17th Aug</td><td>Chq 237415</td><td>682</td><td></td><td>5,321</td></tr>
<tr><td>21st Aug</td><td>CT Tony's TVs</td><td></td><td>4,500</td><td>9,821</td></tr>
<tr><td>21st Aug</td><td>DD Lincoln Council</td><td>787</td><td></td><td>9,034</td></tr>
<tr><td>21st Aug</td><td>DD BCM Ltd</td><td>100</td><td></td><td>8,934</td></tr>
<tr><td>21st Aug</td><td>Bank Charges</td><td>16</td><td></td><td>8,918</td></tr>
<tr><td>21st Aug</td><td>Interest received</td><td></td><td>21</td><td>8,939</td></tr>
<tr><td>CC:</td><td>Cash and cheques</td><td>DD:</td><td colspan="2">Direct Debit</td></tr>
<tr><td>CT:</td><td>Credit transfer</td><td>O/D</td><td colspan="2">Overdrawn</td></tr>
</table>

The cash book as at 22 August is shown below

Date 2015	Details	Bank £	Date 2015	Cheque Number	Details	Bank £
01 Aug	Balance b/f	12,936	3 Aug	237415	Clearvision Ltd	682
21 Aug	Switched On	6,025	3 Aug	237416	P Farnsworth Ltd	542
21 Aug	TVs 4 U	960	7 Aug	237417	Telemagic plc	6,974
22 Aug	Total Entertainment	670	9 Aug	237418	J Baird	377
			17 Aug	237419	C Jenkins	185
			18 Aug	237420	P Goldmark	230

Task 2.18

(a)   Check the items on the bank statement against the items in the cash book
(b)   Update the cash book as needed
(c)   Total the cash book and clearly show the balance carried down at 22nd August (closing balance) AND brought down at 23rd August (opening balance)

Note:
You do not need to adjust the accounts in Section 1.

138

Task 2.18, continued

(d)   **Prepare a bank reconciliation statement as at 24 August.**

Note:
Do not make any entries in the shaded boxes

Bank reconciliation statement as at 24 August 2015	
Balance per bank statement	£
Add:	
Name:	£
Name:	£
Total to add	£
Less:	
Name:	£
Name:	£
Total to subtract	£
Balance as per cash book	£

Task 2.19

You have been asked to prepare a sales invoice for Tony's TVs. Dave's Digital offers this customer a 3% discount for early payment

(a) **Complete the sales invoice below by inserting the net amount, VAT amount and the invoice total.**

DAVE'S DIGITAL

32 Park Street, South Shields, NE33 6TY

Invoice

Number: SV1180
VAT Registration Number 312 6587 41

Invoice to

| Tony's TVs |
| 265 Short Street |
| Dundee |
| DD5 5MY |

Date/ tax point: 1st Sept 2015

Account:

Your reference: 2391

Product Code	Item	Quantity	Price Each	Total
	Scart Leads	6	£ 20.00	
Net Amount				£
VAT @ 20%				£
Invoice Total				£

Terms
    3% settlement discount for settlement within 7 days, other wise 30 days net

Task 2.19, continued

(b)   What will be the amount payable if payment is made within 7 days?

_____

(c)   What will be the amount payable if payment is NOT made within 7 days?

_____

Task 2.20

It is now 30th September 2015. Dave's Digital has received a telephone message from John Baird of Total Entertainment. He tells you that he has received his statement of account which says that he has a credit balance of £50. He wants to know if this means Dave's Digital owes his company some money. You have told him you will look into it for him.

You look into the ledgers and find that the last cheque from Total Entertainment was for £990 rather that £940. You speak to Robert Adler, the Customer Accounts Manager, who agrees you can issue Total Entertainment with a refund cheque. Your supervisor asks you to send them a cheque and write a covering letter.

Using the letterhead on the next page, draft a courteous letter to Mr Baird at Total Entertainment, ready for Robert Adler's signature.

- **State what the problem was and how you are resolving it.**

DAVE'S DIGITAL

32 Park Street,
South Shields,
NE33 6TY

Mr J Baird
Total Entertainment
37 Riverside,
Chester,
CH1 3RD

<u>Answers to Activities</u>

CHAPTER 1

Accounting Roles and Transactions

1.1

a) Bookkeeper
b) Accountant
c) Bookkeeper
d) Accountant
e) Accountant

An accounting technician may cover all of them.

1.2

a) A sole trader owns his/her own business. He/she is personally responsible for any debts and this liability extends beyond the company to his/her own personal assets or savings.
b) A partnership is owned by a group of associated individuals. The partners are jointly responsible for any debts. This liability extends beyond the company to the partners' own personal assets or savings.
c) A limited company is owned by its shareholders. The liability for debts is limited to the assets and savings of the company.

1.3

a) Flat Structure
b) Hierarchical Structure
c) Tall Structure
d) Regional format and a Product format

1.4

a) A list of goods or services sold and given to the purchaser for payment
b) A written acknowledgement that payment has been made for goods or services
c) Businesses which are owned or controlled by the Government
d) The owner(s) of a limited company
e) A book where transactions are first recorded

Chapter 2

Selling Goods and Services

2.1

An estimate is a rough idea of how much a job will cost. It is not legally binding
A quote is a statement of how much a job will cost. It is legally binding.

2.2

- Quotation
- Purchase Order
- Advice Note
- Delivery Note
- Invoice

2.3

c) A bulk discount

2.4

K O'Brian	25 x £3.50 = **£87.50**
L Armstrong	50 x £3.50 = **£175.00**
H Wells	100 x £3.50 = £350.00. Less 10% = £350.00 - £35.00 = **£315.00**
C Perry	60 x £3.50 = **£210.00**
J Booth	75 x £3.50 = £262.50. Less 10% = £262.50 - £26.25 = **£236.25**

2.5

K O'Brian	£87.50 x 20% = **£17.50**	Total = £87.50 + £17.50 = **£105.00**
L Armstrong	£175.00 x 20% = **£35.00**	Total = £175.00 + £35.00 = **£210.00**
H Wells	£315.00 x 20% = **£63.00**	Total = £315.00 + £63.00 = **£378.00**
C Perry	£210.00 x 20% = **£42.00**	Total = £210.00 + £42.00 = **£252.00**
J Booth	£236.25 x 20% = **£47.25**	Total = £236.25 + £47.25 = **£283.50**

2.6

K O'Brian   £87.50 x 2.5% = £2.19
            £87.50 – £2.19 = £85.31
            £85.31 x 20% = **£17.06** (VAT Amount)
            £87.50 + £17.06 = **£104.56** (Invoice Total)

L Armstrong £175.00 x 2.5% = £4.38
             £175.00 – £4.38 = £170.62
             £170.62 x 20% = **£34.12** (VAT Amount)
             £175.00 + £34.12 = **£209.12** (Invoice Total)

H Wells   £315.00 x 2.5% = £7.88
            £315.00 – £7.88 = £307.12
            £307.12 x 20% = **£61.42** (VAT Amount)
            £315.00 + £61.42 = **£376.42** (Invoice Total)

C Perry   £210.00 x 2.5% = £5.25
            £210.00 – £5.25 = £204.75
            £204.75 x 20% = **£40.95** (VAT Amount)
            £210.00 + £40.95 = **£250.95** (Invoice Total)

J Booth   £236.25 x 2.5% = £5.91
            £236.25 – £5.91 = £230.34
            £230.34 x 20% = **£46.06** (VAT Amount)
            £236.25 + £46.06 = **£282.31** (Invoice Total)

2.7

K O'Brian   £104.56 - £2.19 = **£102.37**
L Armstrong £209.12 - £4.38 = **£204.74**
H Wells   £376.42 - £7.88 = **£368.54**
C Perry   £250.95 - £5.25 = **£245.70**
J Booth   £282.31 - £5.91 = **£276.40**

DAWSON SUPPLIES

45 Scartho Street, Immingham, IM15 2BH

Invoice

Number: 35279

Invoice
to

| H Finn |
| 35 Buchanan Place |
| Peterhead |
| AB42 7RG |

Deliver
to

| H Finn |
| 35 Buchanan Place |
| Peterhead |
| AB42 7RG |

Date/ tax point:	1st June 2015
Account:	H Finn
Your reference:	4278
VAT Reg:	GB 369 4928 36

Product Code	Item	Quantity	Price £	Total £
	Speciality Coffee Mugs	100	3.50	350.00
Goods Total				350.00
Trade Discount @ _____%				-
Subtotal				350.00
VAT @ 20%				70.00
Invoice Total				**420.00**

Terms
COD
Ex-works
E&OE

DAWSON SUPPLIES

45 Scartho Street, Immingham, IM15 2BH

Invoice

Number: 35280

Invoice to

| J Harper |
| 67 David Street |
| Barry |
| CF63 2PQ |

Date/ tax point:	1st June 2015
Account:	J Harper
Your reference:	3675
VAT Reg:	GB 369 4928 36

Deliver to

| J Harper |
| 67 David Street |
| Barry |
| CF63 2PQ |

Product Code	Item	Quantity	Price £	Total £
	Speciality Coffee Mugs	150	3.50	525.00
Goods Total				525.00
Trade Discount @ __10_____%				52.50
Subtotal				472.50
VAT @ 20%				94.50
Invoice Total				**567.00**

Terms
COD
Ex-works
E&OE

DAWSON SUPPLIES

45 Scartho Street, Immingham, IM15 2BH

Invoice

Number: 35281

Invoice
to

| T Sawyer |
| 157 Patrick Street |
| Newry |
| BT34 9RY |

Date/ tax point: 1st June 2015

Account: T Sawyer

Your reference: 19735

Deliver
to

| T Sawyer |
| 157 Patrick Street |
| Newry |
| BT34 9RY |

VAT
Reg: GB 369 4928 36

Product Code	Item	Quantity	Price £	Total £
	Speciality Coffee Mugs	144	3.50	504.00
Goods Total				504.00
Trade Discount @ __10_____%				50.40
Subtotal				453.60
VAT @ 20%				88.45
Invoice Total				**542.05**

Terms
COD
Ex-works
E&OE

A settlement discount of 2.5% is offered if paid
within 10 days

(You should ensure you have the correct invoice numbers)

2.9

DAWSON SUPPLIES

45 Scartho Street, Immingham, IM15 2BH

Credit Note

Number: CN357

To

T Sawyer
157 Patrick Street
Newry
BT34 9RY

Date/ tax point:	5th June 2015
Account:	T Sawyer
Your reference:	19735
VAT Reg:	GB 369 4928 36
Our invoice no.	35281

Product Code	Item	Quantity	Price £	Total £
	Speciality Coffee Mugs	12	3.50	42.00
Goods Total				42.00
Trade Discount @ 10%				4.20
Subtotal				37.80
VAT @ 20%				7.37
Credit Total				**45.17**

Reason for Credit
Damaged goods

2.10

STATEMENT OF ACCOUNT
Dawson Supplies

154 Margaret St, Immingham, IM17 9RQ

To

| T Sawyer |
| 157 Patrick Street |
| Newry |
| BT34 9RY |

Account   T Sawyer

Date   30th June 2015

Date	Details	Debit £	Credit £	Balance £
01/06/2012	Balance b/f	525.00		525.00
01/06/2012	Inv 35281	542.05		1067.05
04/06/2012	Chq received		513.83	553.22
04/06/2012	Disc allowed		11.17	542.05
05/06/2012	Credit Note CN357		45.17	496.88
08/06/2012	Chq received		486.48*	10.40
08/06/2012	Disc allowed		10.40*	0.00
26/06/2012	Inv 35396	75.85		75.85

TOTAL AMOUNT OUTSTANDING	75.85

*The discount amount has been reduced to account for discount allowed on 132 mugs rather than 144.

Chapter 3

VAT and Legal Considerations

3.1

a) £50.00

b) No VAT number so no VAT can be recovered. No VAT should be recorded.

c) Under £250 so VAT does not have to be shown separately. VAT amount is £4.37.

d) No VAT. Food and drink is zero rated.

e) Although the VAT amount is wrong, it is the supplier who is responsible for getting it right. You may want to get the supplier to change it, but if you are registered for VAT you can still recover this amount. VAT amount is £112.00.

3.2

1) The offer is when Hannah puts the dress on the counter
(The price shown on the stand is an invitation to treat and not an offer).

2) The acceptance is when the salesperson rings it through the till.

3) The consideration from Hannah is the payment, while the consideration from the salesperson is the dress itself.

4) Hannah is entitled to a refund if she can demonstrate that the wrong size was shown on the label. If, on the other hand, Hannah has grown a size or two after all the Christmas festivities and the label is correct then she has no legal right to a refund (although many shops do offer refunds without a reason having to be given).

5) It may be the shop policy that as a general rule, refunds are not given without a receipt, but if the goods are faulty or not as advertised then a refund can be demanded. However, the shop must have reasonable proof that the goods were bought from this store. Remember that Hannah paid by credit card, so eventually her statement may identify where the goods were bought.

3.3

The contract has been discharged. How it has been discharged will depend on what the agreement actually was.

If the agreement was that the work should be done on that Tuesday then the contract has been discharged by 'frustration'. The plumber couldn't get to Toby's house because the vehicle had broken down.

On the other hand, if it was simply agreed that the plumber would do the job with no specific date then the contract has been discharged by 'agreement'. Toby will get someone else and the plumber has agreed to this.

3.4

a)   As a Sole Trader you are only entitled to a refund.

b)   As a consumer you are entitled to a refund, repair or replacement.

Chapter 4

Recording Sales and Sales Returns

4.1 A collection of interconnected accounts

4.2

a) Invoice or Receipt

b) Sales day Book

c) Sales Ledger or Main Ledger

4.3

SALES DAY BOOK										SDB 97	
Date	Invoice	Customer	Folio	Total		Sales		VAT			
				£	p	£	p	£	p		
2015											
1st May	36597	L Walsh	SL 97	120	00	100	00	20	00		
4th May	36598	C Cole	SL 08	480	00	400	00	80	00		
8th May	36599	S Cowell	SL 12	360	00	300	00	60	00		
15th May	36600	D O'Leary	SL 72	216	00	180	00	36	00		
18th May	36601	D Minogue	SL 58	300	00	250	00	50	00		
22nd May	36602	L Walsh	SL 97	115	20	96	00	19	20		
25th May	36603	D O'Leary	SL 72	14	40	12	00	2	40		
29th May	36604	L Walsh	SL 97	72	00	60	00	12	00		
		TOTAL FOR THE MONTH		1677	60	1398	00	279	60		

4.5

SALES RETURNS DAY BOOK									SRDB 12	
Date	Cr Note	Customer	Folio	Total		Sales Clothes		VAT		
				£	p	£	p	£	p
2015									
11th May	CN 75	S Cowell	SL 12	30	00	25	00	5	00
18th May	CN 76	D O'Leary	SL 72	18	00	15	00	3	00
		TOTAL FOR THE MONTH		48	00	40	00	8	00

4.4, 4.6 & 4.7

SALES LEDGER

Dr	L Walsh Account (SL 97)				Cr
Date	Details	£	Date	Details	£
01/05/15	Inv 36597	120.00	31/05/15	Balance c/d	307.20
22/05/15	Inv 36602	115.20			
29/05/15	Inv 36604	72.00			
		307.20			307.20
01/06/15	Balance b/d	307.20			

Dr	C Cole Account (SL 08)				Cr
Date	Details	£	Date	Details	£
04/05/15	Inv 36598	480.00	31/05/15	Balance c/d	480.00
		480.00			480.00
01/06/15	Balance b/d	480.00			

Dr	S Cowell Account (SL 12)				Cr
Date	Details	£	Date	Details	£
08/05/15	Inv 36599	360.00	11/05/15	CN 75	30.00
			31/05/15	Balance c/d	330.00
		360.00			360.00
01/06/15	Balance b/d	330.00			

Dr	D O'Leary Account (SL 72)				Cr
Date	Details	£	Date	Details	£
15/05/15	Inv 36600	216.00	18/05/15	CN 76	18.00
25/05/15	Inv 36603	14.40	31/05/15	Balance c/d	212.40
		230.40			230.40
01/06/15	Balance b/d	212.40			

Dr	D Minogue Account (SL 58)				Cr
Date	Details	£	Date	Details	£
18/05/15	Inv 36601	300.00	31/05/15	Balance c/d	300.00
		300.00			300.00
01/06/15	Balance b/d	300.00			

MAIN LEDGER

Dr	Sales Account (4000)				Cr
Date	Details	£	Date	Details	£
31/05/15	Balance c/d	1398.00	31/05/15	SDB 97	1398.00
		1398.00			1398.00
			01/06/15	Balance b/d	1398.00

Dr	Sales Returns Account (4050)				Cr
Date	Details	£	Date	Details	£
31/05/15	SRDB 12	40.00	31/05/15	Balance c/d	40.00
		40.00			40.00
01/06/15	Balance b/d	40.00			

156

Dr	VAT Account (2200)				Cr
Date	Details	£	Date	Details	£
31/05/15	SRDB 12	8.00	31/05/15	SDB 97	279.60
31/05/15	Balance c/d	271.60			
		279.60			279.60
			01/06/15	Balance b/d	271.60

Dr	Sales Ledger Control Account (1100)				Cr
Date	Details	£	Date	Details	£
31/05/15	SDB 97	1677.60	31/05/15	SRDB 12	48.00
				Balance c/d	1629.60
		1677.60			1677.60
01/06/15	Balance b/d	1629.60			

4.8

Reconciliation of Sales Ledger Control Account 31st May 2015		
	£	**£**
L Walsh	307.20	
C Cole	480.00	
S Cowell	330.00	
D O'Leary	212.40	
D Minogue	300.00	
TOTAL	**1629.60**	
TOTAL PER SALES LEDGER CONTROL		1629.60
Discrepancy (if any)		nil

Chapter 5

Cash Receipts and Cash Sales

5.1

CASHBOOK - RECEIPTS													**CBR96**	
Date	Detail	Folio	Discount Allowed		Bank		Cash Sale		VAT		Sales Ledger		Other Income	
2015			£	p	£	p	£	p	£	p	£	p	£	p
4th May	Bal b/d				1760	00								
4th May	Cash Sale	ML 4000			257	40	214	50	42	90				
4th May	C Earnshaw	SL25	14	50	565	50					565	50		
4th May	Cash Sale	ML 4000			210	00	175	00	35	00				
4th May	Interest Received	ML 4902			60	00							60	00
4th May	Cash Sale	ML 4000			108	00	90	00	18	00				
4th May	Rent Received	ML 4904			300	00							300	00
4th May	Cash Sale	ML 4000			60	00	50	00	10	00				
4th May	R Lockwood	SL72	16	95	779	70					779	70		
4th May	Cash Sale	ML 4000			69	60	58	00	11	60				
4th May	J Heathcliffe	SL32			881	25					881	25		
			31	45	5051	45	587	50	117	50	2226	45	360	00

5.2

SALES LEDGER

Dr			C Earnshaw Account (SL 25)		Cr
Date	Details	£	Date	Details	£
			04/05/15	CRB 96	565.50
			04/05/15	Disc Allowed	14.50

Dr	J Heathcliffe Account (SL 32)				Cr
Date	Details	£	Date	Details	£
			04/05/15	CRB 96	881.25

Dr	R Lockwood Account (SL 72)				Cr
Date	Details	£	Date	Details	£
			04/05/15	CRB 96	779.70
			04/05/15	Disc Allowed	16.95

MAIN LEDGER

Dr	Sales Account (4000)				Cr
Date	Details	£	Date	Details	£
			04/05/15	CRB 96	587.50

Dr	Interest Received Account (4902)				Cr
Date	Details	£	Date	Details	£
			04/05/15	CRB 96	60.00

Dr	Rent Received Account (4904)				Cr
Date	Details	£	Date	Details	£
			04/05/15	CRB 96	300.00

Dr	VAT Account (2200)				Cr
Date	Details	£	Date	Details	£
			04/05/15	CRB 96	117.50

Dr	Sales Ledger Control Account (1100)				Cr
Date	Details	£	Date	Details	£
			04/05/15	CRB 96	2226.45
			04/05/15	Disc Allowed	31.45

Dr	Discounts Allowed Account (4009)				Cr
Date	Details	£	Date	Details	£
04/05/15	CRB 96	31.45			

5.3

a)   Ask for some other form of payment. The cheque guarantee is per transaction and not per cheque.

b)   There is no date. Fill in the missing date yourself.

c)   The cheque is out of date. Return the cheque and ask for a replacement with the correct date.

d)   The cheque can only be paid into the account of the payee.

5.4

A cheque is drawn on the bank customer's account, whereas a banker's draft is drawn on the bank funds itself. The advantage is that the banker's draft will be paid even if the bank customer does not have sufficient funds.

Chapter 6

Dealing with Banks

6.1

Denomination	Quantity	Total £
£50	0	
£20	7	140.00
£10	15	150.00
£5	11	55.00
£1	25	25.00
50p	5	2.50
20p	45	9.00
10p	52	5.20
5p	25	1.25
2p	36	0.72
1p	11	0.11
		388.78

£338.78 was taken during the day. (Remember the day started with the £50 float)

6.2

Date	6ᵗʰ May 2015		Please detail cheques and slips on the back

Bank Giro Credit

Cashier's stamp

		£	p
£50			
£20		140	00
£10		150	00
£5		25	00
£1		15	00
50p		0	00
Silver		8	45
Bronze		0	33
TOTAL CASH		338	78
Cheque/slips		400	00
£		738	78

IMMINGHAM BANK plc
14 Springfield Road, Brigg, DN20 3GF

Account
D&R Ltd

Paid in by *Your signature*

NUMBER
OF
CHEQUES/
SLIPS   *2*

Sort Code	Account Number
01-26-73	54379654

Paying in slip (front)

Details of cheques/slips	Amount	
	£	p
D Ryder	175	00
G Coulter	225	00
Total cheques/slips carried over	400	00

Paying in slip (back)

6.3

a) A debtor is an individual or company that owes money; a creditor is an individual or company to whom money is owed.

b) Physical possession of personal property is transferred from one person (the 'bailor') to another person (the 'bailee') who subsequently holds possession of the property. However, it is distinguished from a contract of sale or a gift of property, as it only involves the transfer of possession and not its ownership. In order to create a bailment, the bailee must both intend to possess, and actually physically possess, the bailable goods.

c) A Mortgage is the pledging of a property (often a residence) as security for a loan. The mortgagor is the individual or organisation which borrows the money and the mortgagee is the individual or organisation which accepts the mortgage as security.

d) The relation created whereby an individual or organisation (the principal) delegates the transaction of some business activity to another individual or organisation (the agent) which undertakes to carry out the transaction.

6.4

The cheque has to clear through bank clearing system. This usually takes four working days.

6.5

(Five from)

- Cash from customers should be kept in a locked cash box or a till
- The cash in the till should be counted at the end of each day and compared with the till roll
- Cash should be counted by an independent person (i.e. not someone who received the cash)
- Spot checks should be made to ensure all cash is recorded
- Cheques should be recorded on a cash register
- Cash should be taken to the bank daily
- At least two people should take the money to or from the bank
- Money not banked should be kept in a safe and removed from the premises overnight.

Chapter 7

Recording Purchases

7.1 & 7.2

PURCHASES DAY BOOK — **PDB 36**

Date	Invoice	Supplier	Folio	Total		Purchases		Other expenses		VAT	
				£	p	£	p	£	p	£	p
2015											
5th May	53798	I Fleming	PL 17	86	40	72	00			14	40
5th May	36742	T Hardy	PL 21	360	00	300	00			60	00
5th May	2579	A Huxley	PL 23	345	60	288	00			57	60
5th May	36821	E Waugh	PL 58	15	00			12	50	2	50
5th May	68687	D Lawrence	PL 46	90	00	75	00			15	00
5th May	35761	P Wodehouse	PL 61	87	00	72	50			14	50
		TOTAL		984	00	807	50	12	50	164	00

PURCHASES RETURNS DAY BOOK — **PRDB 05**

Date	Cr Note	Supplier	Folio	Total		Purchases returns		Other returns		VAT	
				£	p	£	p	£	p	£	p
2015											
7th May	CN 132	A Huxley	PL 23	14	40	12	00			2	40
7th May	C 268	D Lawrence	PL 46	9	00	7	50			1	50
		TOTAL		23	40	19	50			3	90

PURCHASES LEDGER

Dr				I Fleming Account (PL 17)	Cr
Date	Details	£	Date	Details	£
08/05/15	Balance c/d	86.40	05/05/15	PDB 36	86.40
		86.40			86.40
			09/05/15	Balance b/d	86.40

Dr				T Hardy Account (PL 21)	Cr
Date	Details	£	Date	Details	£
08/05/15	Balance c/d	360.00	05/05/15	PDB 26	360.00
		360.00			360.00
			09/05/15	Balance b/d	360.00

Dr				A Huxley Account (PL 23)	Cr
Date	Details	£	Date	Details	£
07/05/15	PRDB 05	14.40	05/05/15	PDB 36	345.60
08/05/15	Balance c/d	331.20			
		345.60			345.60
			09/05/15	Balance b/d	331.20

Dr				D Lawrence Account (PL 46)	Cr
Date	Details	£	Date	Details	£
07/05/15	PRDB 05	9.00	05/05/15	PDB 36	90.00
08/05/15	Balance c/d	81.00			
		90.00			90.00
			09/05/15	Balance b/d	81.00

Dr				E Waugh Account (PL 58)	Cr
Date	Details	£	Date	Details	£
08/05/15	Balance c/d	15.00	05/05/15	PDB 36	15.00
		15.00			15.00
			09/05/15	Balance b/d	15.00

Dr				P Wodehouse Account (PL 61)	Cr
Date	Details	£	Date	Details	£
08/05/15	Balance c/d	87.00	05/05/15	PDB 36	87.00
		87.00			87.00
			09/05/15	Balance b/d	87.00

MAIN LEDGER

Dr		Purchases				Cr
Date	Details	£	Date	Details		£
05/05/15	PDB 36	807.50	08/05/15	Balance c/d		807.50
		807.50				807.50
09/05/15	Balance b/d	807.50				

Dr		Purchases Returns				Cr
Date	Details	£	Date	Details		£
08/05/15	Balance c/d	19.50	07/05/15	PRDB 05		19.50
		19.50				19.50
			09/05/15	Balance b/d		19.50

Dr		Other expenses				Cr
Date	Details	£	Date	Details		£
05/05/15	PDB 36	12.50	08/05/15	Balance c/d		12.50
		12.50				12.50
09/05/15	Balance b/d	12.50				

Dr		VAT Account				Cr
Date	Details	£	Date	Details		£
05/05/15	PDB 36	164.00	07/05/15	PRDB 05		3.90
			08/05/15	Balance c/d		160.10
		164.00				164.00
09/05/15	Balance b/d	160.10				

Dr		Purchases Ledger Control Account				Cr
Date	Details	£	Date	Details		£
07/05/15	PRDB 05	23.40	05/05/15	PDB 36		984.00
08/05/15	Balance c/d	960.60				
		984.00				984.00
			09/05/15	Balance b/d		960.60

Chapter 8

Making Payments

8.1

PURCHASES DAY BOOK PDB 36

Date	Invoice	Customer	Folio	Total		Purchases		Other expenses		VAT	
				£	p	£	p	£	p	£	p
2015											
1st June	2345	W Sikes	PL 68	180	00	150	00			30	00
5th June	2346	E Corney	PL 27	450	00	375	00			75	00
12th June	2347	E Corney	PL 27	540	00	450	00			90	00
15th June	2348	E Leeford	PL 45	390	00	325	00			65	00
19th June	2349	C Bedwin	PL 03	252	00	210	00			42	00
23rd June	2350	N Claypole	PL 23	900	00	750	00			150	00
26th June	2351	W Sikes	PL 68	300	00	250	00			50	00
		TOTAL		3012	00	2510	00			502	00

PURCHASES RETURNS DAY BOOK PRDB 05

Date	Cr Note	Customer	Folio	Total		Purchases returns		Other returns		VAT	
				£	p	£	p	£	p	£	p
2015											
8th June	17	C Bedwin	PL 03	90	00	75	00			15	00
22nd June	18	F Bumble	PL 06	138	00	115	00			23	00
29th June	19	N Claypole	PL 23	60	00	50	00			10	00
		TOTAL		288	00	240	00			48	00

PURCHASES LEDGER

Dr			C Bedwin Account (PL 03)		Cr
Date	Details	£	Date	Details	£
08/06/15	PRDB 05	90.00	01/06/15	Balance b/d	654.87
30/06/15	Balance c/d	816.87	19/06/15	PDB 36	252.00
		906.87			906.87
			01/07/15	Balance b/d	816.87

Dr			F Bumble Account (PL 06)		Cr
Date	Details	£	Date	Details	£
22/06/15	PRDB 05	138.00	01/06/15	Balance b/d	1672.57
30/06/15	Contra SL	822.50			
30/06/15	Balance c/d	712.07			
		1672.57			1672.57
			01/07/15	Balance b/d	712.07

Dr			N Claypole Account (PL 23)		Cr
Date	Details	£	Date	Details	£
29/06/15	PRDB 05	60.00	01/06/15	Balance b/d	329.64
30/06/15	Balance c/d	1169.64	23/06/15	PDB 36	900.00
		1229.64			1229.64
			01/07/15	Balance b/d	1169.64

Dr			E Corney Account (PL 27)		Cr
Date	Details	£	Date	Details	£
30/06/15	Balance c/d	1365.92	01/06/15	Balance b/d	375.92
			05/06/15	PDB 36	450.00
			12/06/15	PDB 36	540.00
		1365.92			1365.92
			01/07/15	Balance b/d	1365.92

Dr			E Leeford Account (PL 45)		Cr
Date	Details	£	Date	Details	£
30/06/15	Balance c/d	1397.63	01/06/15	Balance b/d	1007.63
			15/06/15	PDB 36	390.00
		1397.63			1397.63
			0107/15	Balance b/d	1397.63

Dr	W Sikes Account (PL 68)				Cr
Date	Details	£	Date	Details	£
30/06/15	Balance c/d	737.92	01/06/15	Balance b/d	257.92
			01/06/15	PDB 36	180.00
			26/06/15	PDB 36	300.00
		737.92			737.92
			01/07/15	Balance c/d	737.92

MAIN LEDGER

Dr	Purchases				Cr
Date	Details	£	Date	Details	£
01/06/15	Balance b/d	23567.57	30/06/15	Balance c/d	26077.57
30/06/15	PDB 36	2510.00			
		26077.57			26077.57
01/07/15	Balance b/d	26077.57			

Dr	Purchases Returns				Cr
Date	Details	£	Date	Details	£
30/06/15	Balance c/d	2266.35	01/06/15	Balance b/d	2026.35
			30/06/15	PRDB 05	240.00
		2266.35			2266.35
			01/07/15	Balance b/d	2266.35

Dr	VAT Account				Cr
Date	Details	£	Date	Details	£
30/06/15	PDB 36	502.00	01/06/15	Balance b/d	1884.85
30/06/15	Balance c/d	1430.85	30/06/15	PRDB 05	48.00
		1932.85			1932.85
			01/07/15	Balance b/d	1430.85

Dr	Purchases Ledger Control Account				Cr
Date	Details	£	Date	Details	£
30/06/15	PRDB 05	288.00	01/06/15	Balance b/d	4298.55
30/06/15	Contra SLC	822.50	30/06/15	PDB 36	3012.00
30/06/15	Balance c/d	6200.05			
		7310.55			7310.55
			01/07/15	Balance b/d	6200.05

Reconciliation of Purchases Ledger Control Account
30th June 2015

	£	£
C Bedwin	816.87	
F Bumble	712.07	
N Claypole	1169.64	
E Corney	1365.92	
E Leeford	1397.63	
W Sikes	737.92	
TOTAL	6200.05	
TOTAL PER PURCHASES LEDGER CONTROL		6200.05
Discrepancy (if any)	nil	

8.2

IMMINGHAM BANK plc
14 Springfield Road, Brigg, DN20 3GF

30 - 25 - 81

Date   29th June 2015

Pay   D MacArthur

Three hundred and six   A/C Payee   pounds   £ 306.00

only

S Craggs

Cheque number	Sort Code	Account number
001481	30-25-81	12560798

IMMINGHAM BANK plc

14 Springfield Road, Brigg, DN20 3GF

30 - 25 – 81

Date *29ᵗʰ June 2015*

Pay *G Patton*

Three hundred and thirty　　A/C Payee　　*pounds*

only

£ | *330.00*

| Cheque number | Sort Code | Account number | S Craggs |
| 001482 | 30-25-81 | 12560798 | |

IMMINGHAM BANK plc

14 Springfield Road, Brigg, DN20 3GF

30 - 25 – 81

Date *29ᵗʰ June 2015*

Pay *R Lee*

Four hundred and twenty　　A/C Payee　　*pounds*

only

£ | *420.00*

| Cheque number | Sort Code | Account number | S Craggs |
| 001483 | 30-25-81 | 12560798 | |

IMMINGHAM BANK plc

14 Springfield Road, Brigg, DN20 3GF

30 - 25 – 81

Date *29ᵗʰ June 2015*

Pay *W Sherman*

One Thousand one hundred　　A/C Payee　　*and*

eleven pounds and 50 pence

£ | *1111.50*

| Cheque number | Sort Code | Account number | S Craggs |
| 001484 | 30-25-81 | 12560798 | |

Explanatory Notes:

A Haig not paid	Over a week before it is due for payment
D MacArthur paid	Already overdue
G Patton paid	Will be over 30 days by next week
R Lee paid	Will be over 30 days by next week
C Gordon not paid	The invoice is already too late to qualify for the settlement discount, but will not be over 30 days next week
J Pershing not paid	Will not be over 30 days next week
T Jackson not paid	Will not be over 30 days next week
W Sherman paid	Will be entitled to settlement discount if paid this week
B Montgomery not paid	Will not be over 30 days next week

8.3

CASHBOOK - PAYMENTS											**CBP83**	
Date	Detail	Discount Received		Bank		Cash Purchases		VAT		Purchases Ledger		Other Expenses	
		£	p	£	p	£	p	£	p	£	p	£	p
01/06/15	Cash purchase (Chq 6735)			150	00	125	00	25	00				
01/06/15	C Dior (Chq 6736)	6	25	286	40					286	40		
02/06/15	Stationery (Chq 6737)			30	00			5	00			25	00
02/06/15	D Dolce (Chq 6738)			552	25					552	25		
02/06/15	Rent (Chq 6739)			450	00							450	00
03/06/15	S Gabbana (Chq 6740)	13	75	630	09					630	09		
04/06/15	Cash purchase (Chq 6741)			96	00	80	00	16	00				
05/06/15	Tea/coffee (Chq 6742)			9	60							9	60
05/06/15	C Klein (Chq 6743)	21	75	996	69					996	69		
05/06/15	Wages (BACS)			1765	36							1765	36
		41	75	4966	39	205	00	46	00	2465	43	2249	96

PURCHASES LEDGER

Dr		C Dior Account			Cr
Date	Details	£	Date	Details	£
01/06/15	CBP 83	286.40			
01/06/15	Disc received	6.25			

Dr		D Dolce Account			Cr
Date	Details	£	Date	Details	£
02/06/15	CBP 83	552.25			

Dr		S Gabbana Account			Cr
Date	Details	£	Date	Details	£
03/06/15	CBP 83	630.09			
03/06/15	Disc received	13.75			

Dr		C Klein Account			Cr
Date	Details	£	Date	Details	£
05/06/15	CBP 83	996.69			
05/06/15	Disc received	21.75			

MAIN LEDGER

Dr		Purchases			Cr
Date	Details	£	Date	Details	£
05/06/15	CBP 83	205.00			

Dr	Other expenses				Cr
Date	Details	£	Date	Details	£
05/06/15	CBP 83	2249.96			

Dr	VAT Account				Cr
Date	Details	£	Date	Details	£
05/06/15	CBP 83	46.00			

Dr	Purchases Ledger Control Account				Cr
Date	Details	£	Date	Details	£
05/06/15	CBP 83	2465.43			
05/06/15	Disc Received	41.75			

Dr	Discounts Received Account				Cr
Date	Details	£	Date	Details	£
			05/06/15	CBP 83	41.75

Chapter 9

Petty Cash

9.1   £127.05

9.2

Petty Cash Voucher No *0698*	
Date prepared *06/06/15*	
Expenditure	**Amount (£)**
Postage Stamps	*8.50*
VAT	*0.00*
TOTAL	£ *8.50*
Paid to _____	
Authorised *A Student*	

Petty Cash Voucher No *0699*	
Date prepared *06/06/15*	
Expenditure	**Amount (£)**
Taxi Fare	*4.75*
VAT	*0.95*
TOTAL	£ *5.70*
Paid to _____	
Authorised *A Student*	

Petty Cash Voucher	No 0700		Petty Cash Voucher	No 0701

Petty Cash Voucher   No 0700

Date prepared   06/06/15

Expenditure	Amount (£)
Train Fare	32.00
VAT	0.00
TOTAL	£ 32.00

Paid to   _____

Authorised   *A Student*

Petty Cash Voucher   No 0701

Date prepared   06/06/15

Expenditure	Amount (£)
Stationery	29.00
VAT	5.80
TOTAL	£ 34.80

Paid to   _____

Authorised   *A Student*

Petty Cash Voucher   No 0702

Date prepared   06/06/15

Expenditure	Amount (£)
Postage	15.60
VAT	0.00
TOTAL	£ 15.60

Paid to   _____

Authorised   *A Student*

Petty Cash Voucher   No 0703

Date prepared   06/06/15

Expenditure	Amount (£)
Taxi fare	6.25
VAT	1.25
TOTAL	£ 7.50

Paid to   _____

Authorised   *A Student*

Petty Cash Voucher	No *0704*	
Date prepared	*06/06/15*	
Expenditure		**Amount (£)**
Taxi fare		*3.75*
VAT		*0.75*
TOTAL	£	*4.50*
Paid to		_____
Authorised		*A Student* _____

Explanatory note:

The laser copier cartridge cannot be paid out of petty cash as it over the maximum limit for petty cash payments. A cheque requisition will need to be completed.

9.3

Petty Cash Book						PCB45									
Receipts		Date	Detail	Voucher Number	Total		Analysis Columns								
							VAT		Travel		Stationery		Postage		
£	p	2015			£	P	£	p	£	p	£	p	£	p
200	00	1st June	Balance b/d											
		1st June	Stamps	0698	8	50							8	50
		2nd June	Taxi	0699	5	70	0	95	4	75				
		2nd June	Train	0700	32	00			32	00				
		3rd June	Stationery	0701	34	80	5	80			29	00		
		3rd June	Postage	0702	15	60							15	60
		3rd June	Taxi	0703	7	50	1	25	6	25				
		5th June	Taxi	0704	4	50	0	75	3	75				
108	60	6th June	Cash Book											
			Balance c/d		200	00								
308	**60**				**308**	**60**	**8**	**75**	**46**	**75**	**29**	**00**	**24**	**10**
200	00	7th June	Balance b/d											

178

Chapter 10

Wages and Salaries

10.1

(a)   £60,000 + £5,362 + £4,200 = £69,562

(b)   £8,379 + £4,608 + £5,362 = £18,349

(c)   £60,000 – £8,379 – £4,608 – £4,200 = £42,813

(d)

Dr	**Wages Expense Account**				Cr
Date	Details	£	Date	Details	£
31/05/15	Wages Control	60,000			
31/05/15	Employer NICs	5,362			
31/05/15	Emp'er Pension	4,200			

Dr	**Wages Control Account**				Cr
Date	Details	£	Date	Details	£
31/05/15	Bank	42,813	31/05/15	Wages Exp	60,000
31/05/15	PAYE	8,379	31/05/15	Employer NICs	5,362
31/05/15	NICs Emp'ee	4,608	31/05/15	Emp'er Pension	4,200
31/05/15	NICs Emp'er	5,362			
31/05/15	Pension Emp'ee	4,200			
31/05/15	Pension Emp'er	4,200			

Dr	**Bank Account**				Cr
Date	Details	£	Date	Details	£
			31/05/15	Net Wages	42,813

Dr	HMRC Account				Cr
Date	Details	£	Date	Details	£
			31/05/15	PAYE	8,379
			31/05/15	NICs Emp'ee	4,608
			31/05/15	NICs Emp'er	5,362

Dr	Pension Fund Account				Cr
Date	Details	£	Date	Details	£
			31/05/15	Pension Emp'ee	4,200
			31/05/15	Pension Emp'er	4,200

10.2

Monday	8 hours @ £12.00	£96.00
Tuesday	8 hours @ £12.00 and 1 hour @ £18.00	£114.00
Wednesday	8 hours @ £12.00 and 2.5 hours @ £18.00	£141.00
Thursday	8 hours @ £12.00 and 0.75 hours @ £18.00	£109.50
Friday	8 hours @ £12.00 and 1.25 hours @ £18.00	£118.50
Total		**£579.00**

Chapter 11

Methods of Communication

11.1

TWO WHEELS

37 South Street,
Salisbury,
SP2 3EQ

On Your Bike
127 St Martin's Street,
Ipswich,
IP1 RQ

2nd June 2015

Dear Mr Jamal

<u>Re Delivery Note 26980</u>

We have received the goods as per the copy delivery note (see enclosed), but you will see from the purchase order (copy also enclosed) that we have received the wrong colour.

We would appreciate your earliest attention to this with a delivery of the bikes of the correct colour, at which time we will return the incorrect items.

Yours sincerely

A Student

A Student
Accounts Assistant

Enc   Copy Purchase Order
       Copy Delivery Note

It is not necessary to have the letter word for word but essential features are the layout, naming the recipient, politeness, concise, the salutation (Yours sincerely) and stating the enclosures. There should be no blame placed on 'On Your Bike'.

Memorandum

To: A Khan

cc: V Symanski

From: A Student

Date: 2nd June 2015

Re: Delivery of Cruiser Bicycles

The delivery of the cruiser bicycles yesterday was of the wrong colour.

'On Your Bike' will be coming with the correct colour (red) and taking back the wrong colour (blue).

I will keep you informed as to the time and date when 'On Your Bike' informs me.

Students should have the correct format and the correct information in a concise manner.

Chapter 12

Less Common Transactions

12.1

CASH BOOK

RECEIPTS   PAYMENTS

Date	Detail	Bank		Date	Detail	Bank	
2015		£		2015		£	
1st June	Capital	100,000	00	1st June	Premises	150,000	00
2nd June	Bank Loan	100,000	00	2nd June	Office equipment	1800	00
5th June	Rental Income	300	00	3rd June	Office fittings	2400	00
5th June	Commission	240	00	3rd June	Advertising	540	00
				4th June	Rates	1000	00
				5th June	Drawings	350	00
				5th June	Loan repayment	5,000	00

Dr		Capital Account			Cr
Date	Details	£	Date	Details	£
			01/06/15	Bank	100,000.00

Dr		VAT Account			Cr
Date	Details	£	Date	Details	£
02/06/15	Bank	300.00	5/06/15	Bank	40.00
03/06/15	Bank	400.00			
03/06/15	Bank	90.00			

Dr		Premises Account			Cr
Date	Details	£	Date	Details	£
01/06/15	Bank	150,000.00			

Dr	Office Fittings Account				Cr
Date	Details	£	Date	Details	£
03/06/15	Bank	2000.00			

Dr	Office Equipment Account				Cr
Date	Details	£	Date	Details	£
02/06/15	Bank	1,500.00			

Dr	Rates Account				Cr
Date	Details	£	Date	Details	£
04/06/15	Bank	1000.00			

Dr	Rent Receivable Account				Cr
Date	Details	£	Date	Details	£
			05/06/15	Bank	300.00

Dr	Bank Loan Account				Cr
Date	Details	£	Date	Details	£
05/06/15	Bank	4808.00	02/06/15	Bank	100,000.00

Dr	Advertising Account				Cr
Date	Details	£	Date	Details	£
03/06/15	Bank	450.00			

Dr	Drawings Account				Cr
Date	Details	£	Date	Details	£
05/06/15	Bank	350.00			

Dr	Commission Account				Cr
Date	Details	£	Date	Details	£
			05/06/15	Bank	200.00

Dr	Interest Paid Account				Cr
Date	Details	£	Date	Details	£
05/06/15	Bank	192.00			

Note: it is equally acceptable to put 'cash book' in place of 'bank' in each of the accounts.

12.2

	Capital Expenditure	Revenue Expenditure
Buying a new property	✓	
Decoration of the new property	✓	
Insurance of property		✓
Purchase of new Vehicle	✓	
Annual Road Fund Licence for vehicle		✓
Fuel for Vehicle		✓
Repair of broken window		✓
Purchase of stock of goods for sale to customers		✓
Purchase of stock of copy paper for the photocopier		✓
New machine for the factory	✓	
Delivery cost of the machine	✓	
12 months service agreement on the machine		✓

12.3

Account name	Debit £	Credit £
Bad Debt account	3,800	
VAT account	760	
Sales Ledger Control		4,560

The individual customer account will need crediting with £4,560 to write off this amount in the individual customer account.

Chapter 13

The Cash Book and Bank Statement

13.1 & 13.2

CASH BOOK

RECEIPTS   PAYMENTS

Date	Detail	Bank		Date	Detail	Bank	
2015		£		2015		£	
1st June	Balance b/d	2,856	29	1st June	C Wren Chq 2398	253	60
1st June	Receipt from F L Wright	587	50	5th June	Stationery Chq 2399	30	00
12th June	Receipt from J Nash	528	72	8th June	Telephone Chq 2400	174	32
15th June	Cash receipt for inv 23699	58	79	15th June	C Barry Chq 2401	172	50
15th June	Receipt from W Lamb	563	50	19th June	Rent Chq 2402	400	00
30th June	Receipt from G Scott	310	00	26th June	Wages by BACS	2798	56
25th June	M D Sully BACS receipt	135	50	30th June	Rates Chq 2403	500	00
				16th June	Pei Hire Company Direct Debit	50	00
				30th June	Bank Charges	13	50
				30th June	Balance c/d	647	82
		5040	30			5040	30
1st July	Balance b/d	647	82				

13.3

```
+-----------------------------------------------------------------+
|              Bank Reconciliation Statement                      |
|                    30 June 2015                                 |
|                                                                 |
|                                         £              £        |
|                                                                 |
| Balance as per bank statement                        837.82     |
|                                                                 |
| Less: unpresented cheques                                       |
|                                                                 |
|        2403                           500.00                    |
|                                                                 |
|                                                      _____     |
|                                                      337.82     |
|                                                                 |
| Add: outstanding lodgements                                     |
|                                                                 |
|                                       310.00                    |
|                                                                 |
|                                                      _____     |
|                                                                 |
|                                                                 |
| Balance as per cash book                             647.82     |
|                                                                 |
+-----------------------------------------------------------------+
```

Chapter 14

Journals and the Trial Balance

14.1

Date	Details	Dr	Cr
2015 1st June		£	£
	Bank Account	6,500	
	Vehicle Account	4,000	
	Cash Account	200	
	Office Equipment Account	350	
	Stock	500	
	Capital Account		11,550
	Being the opening assets introduced into the business		

(Students may have shown each item in a separate journal)

14.2

(a)

Dr			Sales Ledger Control Account		Cr
Date	Details	£	Date	Details	£
01/06/15	Balance b/d	57,001	30/06/15	Receipts from debtors	102,523
30/06/15	Credit Sales	96,478	30/06/15	Discounts allowed	2,055
			30/06/15	Sales Returns	5,250
			30/06/15	Balance c/d	43,651
		153,479			153,479
01/07/15	Balance b/d	43,651			

189

(b)

Reconciliation of Sales Ledger Control Account 30th June 2015		
	£	£
W Blake	8,295	
J Constable	10,428	
T Gainsborough	6,220	
F Hals	3,555	
H Holbein	9,269	
W Turner	3,275	
TOTAL	41,042	
TOTAL PER SALES LEDGER CONTROL		43,651
Discrepancy (if any)		2609

(c)

Date	Details	Dr	Cr
2015		£	£
30th June	Bad Debt expense	2609	
	Sales Ledger Control		2609
	Being the write off of the amount owed to us by J Pollock		

14.3

	Trial Balance 30th June 2015		
		Dr £	Cr £
Name of account			
Sales			113,820
Sales Returns		2,334	
Purchases		63,000	
Purchase Returns			1,850
Sales Ledger Control		6,669	
Purchases Ledger Control			5,656
Office Equipment		28,875	
Vehicles		20,000	
Stock		8,175	
Cash		892	
Wages		20,680	
General expenses		21,713	
Bank			2,215
Bank Loan			5,000
VAT			864
Drawings		20,000	
Capital			63,000
Suspense		67	
		192,405	**192,405**

14.4

Date	Details	Dr	Cr
2015		£	£
30th	Sales Ledger Control	576	
June	Sales		480
	VAT		96
	Being omission of Sales Invoice		

Date	Details	Dr	Cr
2015 30th June	Bank	£ 805	£
	Sales Ledger Control		805
	Being omission of cheque from customer		

Date	Details	Dr	Cr
2015 30th June	General Expenses	£ 120	£
	Suspense account		120
	Being omission of recording Road Fund Licence in General Expense account		

Date	Details	Dr	Cr
2015 30th June	Sales	£ 520	£
	VAT	104	
	Sales Ledger Control		624
	Being correction of recording sales invoice twice		

Date	Details	Dr	Cr
2015 30th June	Suspense	£ 20	£
	Bank		20
	Being correction of incorrect figure in cash book		

Date	Details	Dr	Cr
2015 30th June	Drawings	£ 200	£
	Purchases		200
	Being goods take by owner for own use		

Date	Details	Dr	Cr
2015 30th June	Suspense	£ 33	£
	Bank		33
	Being omission of bank charges from the cash book		

Dr	Suspense Account				Cr
Date	Details	£	Date	Details	£
30/06/15	TB Difference	67	30/06/15	General expenses	120
30/06/15	Bank	20			
30/06/15	Bank	33			
		120			120

14.5

Trial Balance (Amended)
30th June 2015

Name of account	Dr £	Cr £
Sales		113,780
Sales Returns	2,334	
Purchases	62,800	
Purchase Returns		1,850
Sales Ledger Control	5,816	
Purchases Ledger Control		5,656
Office Equipment	28,875	
Vehicles	20,000	
Stock	8,175	
Cash	892	
Wages	20,680	
General expenses	21,833	
Bank		1,463
Bank Loan		5,000
VAT		856
Drawings	20,200	
Capital		63,000
Suspense		
	191,605	**191,605**

14.6

SALES LEDGER

Dr	L C Brown Account				Cr
Date	Details	£	Date	Details	£
30/06/15	Balance b/d	6,749	30/06/15	Cash Book	3,450
30/06/15	SDB	720	30/06/15	Disc Allowed	75
			30/06/15	Balance c/d	3,944
		7469			7469
01/07/15	Balance b/d	3,944			

Dr	P Thrower Account				Cr
Date	Details	£	Date	Details	£
30/06/15	Balance b/d	1,628	30/06/15	SRDB	192
30/06/15	SDB	480	30/06/15	Cash Book	750
			30/06/15	Balance c/d	1,166
		2,108			2,108
01/07/15	Balance b/d	1,166			

Dr	A Titchmarsh Account				Cr
Date	Details	£	Date	Details	£
30/06/15	Balance b/d	5,796	30/06/15	SRDB	48
30/06/15	SDB	1,200	30/06/15	Balance c/d	6,948
		6,996			6,996
01/07/15	Balance b/d	6,948			

Dr	C Dimmock Account				Cr
Date	Details	£	Date	Details	£
30/06/15	Balance b/d	2,150	30/06/15	Balance c/d	2,774
30/06/15	SDB	624			
		2,774			2,774
01/07/15	Balance b/d	2,774			

Dr	J Loudon Account				Cr
Date	Details	£	Date	Details	£
30/06/15	Balance b/d	336	30/06/15	Bad debt	336
		336			336

MAIN LEDGER

Dr			Sales Account		Cr
Date	Details	£	Date	Details	£
30/06/15	Balance c/d	183,274	30/06/15	Balance b/d	180,754
			30/06/15	SDB	2,520
		183,274			183,274
			01/07/15	Balance b/d	183,274

Dr			Sales Ledger Control Account		Cr
Date	Details	£	Date	Details	£
30/06/15	Balance b/d	16,659	30/06/15	SRDB	240
30/06/15	SDB	3,024	30/06/15	Cash Book	4,200
			30/06/15	Disc Allowed	75
			30/06/15	Journal	336
			30/06/15	Balance c/d	14,832
		19,683			19,683
01/07/15	Balance b/d	14,832			

Dr			Sales Returns Account		Cr
Date	Details	£	Date	Details	£
30/06/15	Balance b/d	1,748	30/06/15	Balance c/d	1,948
30/06/15	SRDB	200			
		1,948			1,948
01/07/15	Balance b/d	1,948			

Dr			Discounts Allowed Account		Cr
Date	Details	£	Date	Details	£
30/06/15	Balance b/d	405	30/06/15	Balance c/d	480
30/06/15	SLC	75			
		480			480
01/07/15	Balance b/d	480			

Dr			Office Expenses Account		Cr
Date	Details	£	Date	Details	£
30/06/15	Balance b/d	1,680	30/06/15	Balance c/d	1,880
30/06/15	Journal	80			
30/06/15	Journal	120			
		1,880			1,880
01/07/15	Balance b/d	1,880			

Dr			Wages Expense Account		Cr
Date	Details	£	Date	Details	£
30/06/15	Balance b/d	32,232	30/06/15	Journal	120
30/06/15	Cash Book	3,200	30/06/15	Balance c/d	35,312
		35,432			35,432
01/07/15	Balance b/d	35,312			

Dr	VAT Account				Cr
Date	Details	£	Date	Details	£
30/06/15	SRDB	40	30/06/15	Balance b/d	1,470
30/06/15	Journal	56	30/06/15	SDB	504
30/06/15	Journal	16			
30/06/15	Balance c/d	1,862			
		1,974			1,974
			01/07/15	Balance b/d	1,862

Dr	Bad Debts Account				Cr
Date	Details	£	Date	Details	£
30/06/15	Balance b/d	208	30/09/15	Balance c/d	488
30/06/15	Journal	280			
		488			488
01/07/15	Balance b/d	488			

Dr	Suspense Account				Cr
Date	Details	£	Date	Details	£
30/06/15	Balance b/d	96	30/06/15	Journal	96
		96			96

Date	Details	Dr	Cr
2015 30th June		£	£
	Bad Debt	280	
	VAT	56	
	Sales Ledger Control		336
	Being write off of bad debt re J Louden		
Date	Details	Dr	Cr
2015 30th June		£	£
	Office Expenses	80	
	VAT	16	
	Suspense		96
	Being correction of posting error		

Date	Details	Dr	Cr
2015		£	£
30th June	Office Expenses	120	
	Wages		120
	Being correction of error of commission		

14.7

Trial Balance
30th June 2015

Name of account	Dr £	Cr £
Premises	250,000	
Motor vehicles	30,000	
Office Equipment	10,460	
Stock	7,487	
Bank	423	
Cash	250	
Sales Ledger Control	14,832	
Purchases Ledger Control		6,559
VAT		1,862
Drawings	25,042	
Capital		283,000
Sales		183,274
Sales Returns	1,948	
Discounts Allowed	480	
Purchases	97,686	
Purchases Returns		1,551
Discounts Received		377
Rent Received		7,500
Wages	35,312	
Office Expenses	1,880	
Motor Expenses	1,050	
Heat & Light	2,526	
Bad Debts	488	
Rates	3,860	
Bank charges	399	
Suspense	0	
	484,123	**484,123**

14.8

a) Assets $300000 + 20000 + 10000 + 6000 + 25000 = 361000$
    Liabilities $30000 + 15000 = 45000$
    Capital 316000

b) $361000 - 45000 = 316000$

c) $363000 - 47000 = 316000$

PRACTICE EXAMINATION 1
Martin's Mobiles

Task 1.1

Date 2015	Details	Invoice number	Total £	VAT £	Net £
31 July	**Capital Communications**	2786	2,160	360	1,800
31 July	**Mobile Mania**	2787	1,008	168	840
31 July	**The Mobile Box**	2788	4,320	720	3,600
31 July	**Keep Talking**	2789	1,872	312	1,560
Total			9,360	1,560	7,800

Task 1.2
(a)
Subsidiary (sales) ledger

Account name	Amount £	Debit ✓	Credit ✓
Capital Communications	2,160	✓	
Mobile Mania	1,008	✓	
The Mobile Box	4,320	✓	
Keep Talking	1,872	✓	

(b)
Main ledger

Account name	Amount £	Debit ✓	Credit ✓
Sales Ledger Control Account	9,360	✓	
Sales Account	7,800		✓
VAT Account	1,560		✓

Task 1.3

Main ledger

Account name	Amount £	Debit ✔	Credit ✔
Purchases	13,160	✔	
VAT	2,632	✔	
Purchases Ledger Control	15,792		✔

Task 1.4

Main ledger

Account name	Amount £	Debit ✔	Credit ✔
Purchases Ledger Control	4,512	✔	
Purchases Returns	3,760		✔
VAT	752		✔

Task 1.5

Main ledger

Account name	Amount £	Debit ✔	Credit ✔
Cash book	2,112	✔	
Sales	1,760		✔
VAT	352		✔

Task 1.6

(a)

Subsidiary (sales) ledger

Account name	Amount £	Debit ✓	Credit ✓
The Mobile Box	14,582		✓
The Mobile Box	317		✓
Keep Talking	3,290		✓

(b)

Main ledger

Account name	Amount £	Debit ✓	Credit ✓
Discounts allowed	317	✓	
Sales Ledger Control	317		✓
Sales Ledger Control	17,872		✓

Task 1.7

Office expenses

Date 2015	Details	Amount £	Date 2015	Details	Amount £
1 July	Balance b/d	1,650	31 July	Journal	80
15 July	Cash book	1,965	31 July	Balance c/d	3,535
		3,615			3,615
1 Aug	Balance b/d	3,535			

Task 1.8

Main ledger

Account name	Amount £	Debit ✓	Credit ✓
Purchases Ledger Control	1,250	✓	
Sales Ledger Control	1,250		✓

Task 1.9

(a)

Account name	Amount £	Debit ✓	Credit ✓
Suspense account	300	✓	
Discounts received	300		✓
Suspense account	300	✓	
Discounts received	300		✓

(b)

Account name	Amount £	Debit ✓	Credit ✓
Motor expenses	350	✓	
Motor vehicles	350		✓

(c)

Account name	Amount £	Debit ✓	Credit ✓
Bad Debt	1880	✓	
VAT	376	✓	
Sales Ledger Control	2256		✓

Task 1.10

Account name	Amount £	Debit £	Credit £
Premises	200,000	200,000	
Motor Vehicles	15,000	15,000	
Office Equipment	7.600	7,600	
Stock	7,460	7,460	
Bank (debit balance)	2.579	2,579	
Sales Ledger Control	19,645	19,645	
Purchases Ledger Control	18,790		18,790
VAT (credit balance)	674		674
Drawings	15,250	15,250	
Capital	196,000		196,000
Sales	143,395		143,395
Sales Returns	685	685	
Discounts Allowed	114	114	
Purchases	89,535	89,535	
Purchases Returns	1,495		1,495
Discounts Received	185		185
Rent Received	2,500		2,500
Wages & Salaries	4,425	4,425	
Office expenses	524	524	
Petty Cash	250	250	
Miscellaneous expenses	63	63	
Suspense account (credit balance)	91		91
TOTALS		363,130	363,130

Task 2.1

(a) **By what date should you instruct your bank to pay this amount in order for it to reach The Phone Shed by this date?**

Wednesday 29th July.

(b) **Give ONE advantage of paying in this way.**

One from:

Quicker
Cheaper
More secure

(c) **Will Martin's Mobiles be shown as a debtor or creditor in The Phone Shed's accounts?**

(Debtor) / Creditor

Task 2.2

(a) **Suggest an appropriate four-character alpha-numeric ledger code for this account.**

One from:

UP30
UL30
SL30

(b) **In which ledger would you expect to see this account?**

	✓
Main ledger	
Subsidiary Sales ledger	✓
Subsidiary Purchases ledger	

Task 2.3

Date 2015	Details	Amount £	Date 2015	Details	Total £	Stationery £	Postage £	Travel £
1 July	Balance b/f	100	10 July	Postage Stamps	36		36	
			17 July	Pens	10	10		
			24 July	Taxi fare	7			7
			31 July	Envelopes	12	12		
			31 July	Balance c/f	35			
	Total	100		Total	100	22	36	7
1 Aug	Balance b/f	35						

(d) **What amount will be required to restore the imprest level to £100?**

£65

Task 2.4

1	Voucher has not yet been recorded
2	There has been an error in calculation
3	There has been a theft from the petty cash box

Task 2.5

(a) £10,277.00

(b) £6283.00

(c) £3994.00

(d) Payable to HM Revenue & Customs

Task 2.6

Martin's Mobiles is considering buying a new delivery vehicle. Your supervisor is wondering whether he could ask the bank for an overdraft.

(a)   What is an overdraft?

A Form of borrowing where the current account can be overdrawn up to an agreed amount.

(b)   Would the overdraft show in the trial balance at Martin's mobiles as a debit or a credit balance?

Debit   /   (Credit)

Task 2.7

What document would you send or receive in the following circumstances?

		✓
To accompany a cheque to your supplier	Receipt	
	Delivery Note	
	Remittance Advice	✓

		✓
To advise the customer of amounts outstanding and already paid	Statement	✓
	Delivery Note	
	Invoice	

		✓
To advise a customer that an order has been received	Receipt	
	Advice note	✓
	Remittance Advice	

Task 2.8

Complete the following sentences by inserting the relevant legal terms

(a)   A price shown on the supermarket shelf is called   *an invitation to treat*

(b)   For a contract to exist there must be an intention to create legal relations, an agreement, and a   *consideration*

(c)   A contract is said to be discharged through agreement, frustration, breach of contract or   *performance*

Task 2.9

(a)   £1,467

(b)   £576

(c)   £2,243

Task 2.10

Would each of the following be a debit or credit entry in the Wages and Salaries control account in the Main ledger?

Account name	Debit ✔	Credit ✔
Net wages paid to employees	✔	
Employee's pension contribution	✔	
Employee's NIC	✔	
Gross Wages		✔

Task 2.11

Apart from invoices charged to the customer name THREE other items which may be found on a statement of account.

1	Credit notes
2	Discounts allowed
3	Payments from the customer

Task 2.12

Martin's Mobile customers can pay by debit card or credit card if they wish to purchase a phone over the internet or by phone.

(a)   **Briefly explain the difference between a debit card and a credit card.**

Debit cards are linked directly to the customer's bank account. Amounts will be taken from the account immediately

Credit card payments are noted to the customer's credit card provider and a statement will be sent monthly. The customer can then choose to pay off the whole amount or to pay only part of the bill.

(b)   **Name THREE credit card details the customer will be asked for when payment is taken over the phone.**

1	Card Number
2	Expiry Date
3	Security number on reverse of card

(Alternatives are: Name on card, start date, the kind of card e.g. VISA, American Express etc, issue number)

Task 2.13

(a)   Give THREE reasons why the cheque cannot be paid by Immingham Bank

1	The cheque is out of date (the date is more than 6 months ago)
2	The amounts in figures and words don't match
3	It is not signed

(b)   What does the 'A/C Payee' crossing mean?

The cheque can only be paid into the account of Martin's Mobiles

(c)   If the date were missing from the cheque altogether could Martin's Mobiles fill this in themselves?

 Yes / No

Task 2.14

Martin's Mobiles is considering offering discounts customers to boost trade.

What is the name of the discount for:

	Settlement Discount ✓	Bulk Discount ✓	Trade Discount ✓
A 10% discount for orders over £1,000		✓	
A 3% discount for payment within 10 days	✓		
A 15% discount to other mobile phone traders			✓

Task 2.15

When customers pay cash, the money is kept in the till until Friday afternoon when your supervisor takes it to the bank on his way home. He quickly counts the money before he leaves for the bank. There is often more the £1,000 to bank.

Suggest THREE changes that could be made to improve security

Three from:

Bank the cash daily

Keep cash in a safe overnight

Vary the times of going to the bank

Ensure that two people check the amount to be banked

Ensure at least two people take the money to the bank

Check the amount with the till roll

Use a security firm

Task 2.16

Martin's Mobiles' transactions in July included the items listed below.

State whether each is a capital transaction or a revenue transaction

Transaction	Capital or Revenue
Annual decoration of office	Revenue
Purchase of a new computer	Capital
Repair of broken window	Revenue
Wages paid to employees	Revenue

Task 2.17

This is a summary of transactions with customers during July

(a) **Show whether each entry will be a debit or credit in the Sales ledger control account in the Main Ledger.**

Account name	Amount £	Debit ✓	Credit ✓
Balance of debtors at 1st July 2015	18,129	✓	
Goods sold on credit (inclusive of VAT)	7,656	✓	
Money received from credit customers	6,085		✓
Discounts allowed	35		✓
Goods returned by credit customers (inclusive of VAT)	20		✓

(b) **What will be the balance brought down on 1st August on the above account?** ✓

Dr £19,645	✓
Cr £19,645	
Dr £19,575	
Cr £19,575	
Dr £16,613	
Cr £16,613	

Task 2.17, continued

The following opening balances were in the subsidiary sales ledger on 1 August:

Capital Communications £4,744 debit
Eezee Phone £346 credit
Keep Talking £3,824 debit
Mobile Mania £987 debit
The Mobile Box £9,744 debit

(c)   Reconcile the balances shown above with the sales ledger control account balance you have calculated in part (b)

	£
Sales ledger control account balance as at 1 August	**19,645**
Total of subsidiary sales ledger accounts as at 1 August	**18,953**
Difference	**692**

The sales ledger control account and the subsidiary sales ledger do not agree.

(d)   What may have caused the difference?

The subsidiary sales ledger amount for Eezee Phone could have been a debit balance

Task 2.18

Date 2015	Details	Bank £	Date 2015	Cheque Number	Details	Bank £
01 July	Balance b/f	1,733	5 July	001484	Digiphones	2,450
10 July	Eezee Phone	1,250	8 July	001485	NGJ Ltd	199
15 July	Mobile Mania	1,500	8 July	001486	P Erskine	88
17 July	**The Mobile Box**	**4,750**	11 July	001487	T Alexander Ltd	250
24 July	**Keep Talking**	**1750**	15 July	001488	A Sarin	126
24 July	**Interest Received**	**5**	15 July	001489	E Richards	75
			22 July		Happy Talk Phones	1,560
			23 July		**The Phone Shed**	**175**
			24 July		**Bank Charges**	**37**
			24 July		**Balance c/d**	**6,028**
		10,988				10,988
25 July	**Balance b/d**	**6,028**				

Bank reconciliation statement as at 24 July 2015	
Balance per bank statement	£ 3,492
Add:	
Name: **Eezee Phone**	£ 1,250
Name: **Mobile Mania**	£ 1,500
Total to add	£ 2,750
Less:	
Name: **P Erskine (Chq 001486)**	£ 88
Name: **A Sarin (Chq 001488)**	£ 126
Total to subtract	£ 214
Balance as per cash book	£ 6,028

Task 2.19

Date 01 August 2015	Lindum Bank plc Lincoln	£50 notes	
		£20 notes	
		£10 notes	£40.00
	Account Martin's Mobiles	£5 notes	£30.00
		£2 coin	£26.00
		£1 coin	£12.00
	Paid in by *Martin Butler*	Other coin	£3.50
		Total cash	£111.50
		Cheques, POs	£4680.00
	09-26-54 23975618	Total £	£4791.50

Task 2.20

MARTIN'S
MOBILES

225 Park Road,
Lincoln,
LN6 3WD

Mr W Cooke
Capital Communications
Kilburn High Road,
London,
NW2 3RT

31st July 2015

Dear Sir

Invoice 3567

Further to our previous reminder, we still have not received settlement of the overdue invoice. The amount outstanding is £4,744 on invoice 3567 dated 24th April 2012. We enclose a copy for your information. We shall be grateful if you will kindly forward us your cheque in full payment of this account. If this amount has not been received by return of post we will have no alternative but to place the matter in the hands of our solicitors.

Yours faithfully

Mr Martin Butler
Martin's Mobiles

Encl.   Copy invoice 3567

PRACTICE EXAMINATION 2
Dave's Digitals

Task 1.1

(a)

Subsidiary (purchases) ledger

Account name	Amount £	Debit ✓	Credit ✓
Clearvision Ltd	6,240		✓
Telemagic plc	1,440		✓
Sound & Vision Ltd	816		✓
Tipachi plc	2,400		✓

(b)

Main ledger

Account name	Amount £	Debit ✓	Credit ✓
Purchases	9,080	✓	
VAT	1,816	✓	
Purchases ledger control	10,896		✓

Task 1.2

Date 2015	Details	Invoice number	Total £	VAT £	Net £
31 July	Tony's TVs	5369	3,360	560	2,800
31 July	TVs 4 U	5370	768	128	640
31 July	Switched On	5371	10,224	1,704	8,520
31 July	Total Entertainment	5372	864	144	720
Total			15,216	2,536	12,680

Task 1.3

(a)

Subsidiary (sales) ledger

Account name	Amount £	Debit ✓	Credit ✓
Tony's TVs	3,360	✓	
TVs 4 U	768	✓	
Switched On	10,224	✓	
Total Entertainment	864	✓	

(b)

Main ledger

Account name	Amount £	Debit ✓	Credit ✓
Sales ledger control	15,216	✓	
Sales	12,680		✓
VAT	2,536		✓

Task 1.4

(a)

Subsidiary (purchases) ledger

Account name	Amount £	Debit ✓	Credit ✓
Clearvision Ltd	96	✓	
Tipachi plc	240	✓	

(b)

Main ledger

Account name	Amount £	Debit ✓	Credit ✓
Purchases returns	280		✓
VAT	56		✓
Purchases ledger control	336	✓	

Task 1.5

Main ledger

Account name	Amount £	Debit ✓	Credit ✓
Cash Book	2,256	✓	
Sales	1,880		✓
VAT	376		✓

Task 1.6

Subsidiary (sales) ledger

Account name	Amount £	Debit ✓	Credit ✓
Switched On	3,563		✓
Switched On	138		✓

Subsidiary (purchases) ledger

Account name	Amount £	Debit ✓	Credit ✓
Tipachi plc	1,260	✓	

Main ledger

Account name	Amount £	Debit ✓	Credit ✓
Sales ledger control	3,563		✓
Sales ledger control	138		✓
VAT	197		✓
Purchases ledger control	1,260	✓	
Office Equipment	1,000	✓	
Rent	825	✓	
Telephone	120	✓	
Petty cash	150	✓	
Discounts Allowed	138	✓	
VAT	191	✓	

Task 1.7

Petty Cash Control

Date 2015	Details	Amount £	Date 2015	Details	Amount £
1 Aug	Balance b/d	200	31 Aug	Petty Cash Book	150
31 Aug	Bank	150	31 Aug	Balance c/d	200
		350			350
1 Sept	Balance b/d	200			

Task 1.8

(a) An amount of £75 has been debited to the miscellaneous expenses account instead of the motor expenses account.

Account name	Amount £	Debit ✓	Credit ✓
Motor expenses	75	✓	
Miscellaneous expenses	75		✓

(b) Purchases returns of £200 have been entered as £2,000 in the Main ledger accounts (ignore VAT)

Account name	Amount £	Debit ✓	Credit ✓
Purchases returns	1,800	✓	
Purchases ledger control	1.800		✓

Task 1.8, continued

(c)   A credit customer, JD's Ltd, has ceased trading. It owes Dave's Digital £1,760 plus VAT. The net amount and the VAT must be written off in the Main ledger.

Account name	Amount £	Debit ✓	Credit ✓
Bad debt	1,760	✓	
VAT	352	✓	
Sales ledger control	2,112		✓

Task 1.9

Account name	Amount £	Debit ✓	Credit ✓
Suspense	132	✓	
Discounts received	132		✓
Motor expenses	9	✓	
Suspense	9		✓

Task 1.10

Account name	Amount £	Debit £	Credit £
Motor Vehicles	16,212	16,212	
Office Equipment	17,572	17,572	
Stock	30,560	30,560	
Bank (debit balance)	6,784	6,784	
Petty cash control	200	200	
Sales Ledger Control	163,257	163,257	
Purchases Ledger Control	119,415		119,415
VAT owing	22,719		22,719
Capital	29,129		29,129
Sales	611,974		611,974
Sales Returns	458	458	
Discounts Allowed	336	336	
Discounts Received	372		372
Purchases	472,160	472,160	
Purchases Returns	4,759		4,759
Wages	69,372	69,372	
Travel expenses	2,946	2,946	
Motor expenses	1,572	1,572	
Office expenses	4,770	4,770	
Bad Debts	1,222	1,222	
Miscellaneous expenses	947	947	
TOTALS		788,368	788,368

Task 2.1

(a) **What is an imprest system?**

The petty cashier starts each week or month with a fixed amount of money

(b) **Complete the following reconciliation**

Petty cash reconciliation	£	p
Balance on petty cash control account	50	00
Cash in hand	45	50
Difference	4	50

(c) **Suggest THREE possible reasons for the difference**

Any three from

1) A voucher has not been recorded

2) Money has been borrowed from the tin

3) Money has been stolen from the tin

4) There has been a recording error in the petty cash book

Task 2.2

(a) Complete the VAT calculation summary below.

	VAT amount £
Sales £262,280 **excluding** VAT	52,456
Purchases £237,726 **including** VAT	39,621
VAT Payable	12,835

(b) What will be the accounting entries required to record payment of this amount by cheque?

Account name	Debit ✓	Credit ✓
VAT	✓	
Cash Book		✓

Task 2.3

(a) What is the amount to be paid to Sound & Vision Ltd?

£419.04

(b) What is the purpose of a TRADE discount?

	✓
To reward customers who pay in cash	
To offer a lower price to an organisation within the same trade	✓
To reduce the price of goods which are damaged	

Task 2.3, continued

(c) **To which customers might Dave's Digital offer a BULK discount?**

	✓
Those placing large orders	✓
Those with many branches	
Those who have been customers for many years	

Task 2.4

What document would you send or receive in the following circumstances?

		✓
To adjust the customer's account for goods returned	Invoice	
	Credit Note	✓
	Remittance Advice	

		✓
To accompany and list the goods ordered	Statement	
	Delivery Note	✓
	Receipt	

		✓
To acknowledge payment for goods	Receipt	✓
	Advice note	
	Remittance Advice	

Task 2.5

The following errors have been made in the accounts of Dave's Digital.

Show whether the errors cause an imbalance by selecting the correct answer

(a) **Discount allowed has not been taken by a customer**

	✓
The trial balance will balance	✓
The trial balance will not balance	

(b) **A purchase invoice has been entered correctly in the main ledger, but omitted from the subsidiary purchases ledger.**

	✓
The trial balance will balance	✓
The trial balance will not balance	

(c) **A payment for service to a vehicle has been entered into the miscellaneous expenses instead of the motor expenses.**

	✓
The trial balance will balance	✓
The trial balance will not balance	

(d) **A cash purchases has been entered into the cash book but not into the purchases account or the VAT account.**

	✓
The trial balance will balance	
The trial balance will not balance	✓

Task 2.5, continued

(e)   VAT on a Sales invoice has been incorrectly calculated

	✓
The trial balance will balance	✓
The trial balance will not balance	

Task 2.6

Dave's Digital gives all stock items a code number when it arrives.

(a)   Explain why this is done.

The correct item can be found more easily and more accurately.

Task 2.7

A cheque has been received by Dave's Digital dated 27th August 2014 and the bank will not accept it.

(a)   Explain why

A cheque is out of date after 6 months

(b)   If a cheque was paid into the bank on Monday morning, when can you be certain a withdrawal be made against that cheque?

Friday (after 4 working days)

Task 2.8

On 1 August Dave's Digital offered to supply some goods to a customer. The customer posted the acceptance on 3 August and it was received at Dave's Digital on 6 August.

What is the date on which the contract was formed?

	✔
1 August	
3 August	✔
6 August	

Task 2.9

Which TWO items would you expect to see in a Wages and salaries control account?

	✔
Gross wages paid to employees	✔
Drawings by the owner of the business	
Payment to 'Office Clean Ltd' for cleaning the office	
Payment by the employee to a trade union	✔
Payment to creditors	

Task 2.10

Dave's Digital's transactions in August included the items listed below.

State whether each is a capital transaction or a revenue transaction

Transaction	Capital or Revenue
Replacement of a worn tyre on a delivery vehicle	**Revenue**
Purchase goods for resale	**Revenue**
Purchase of new vehicle	**Capital**
12 months' road fund licence for the new vehicle	**Revenue**

Task 2.11

Dave's Digital makes use of the BACS system for making payments.

Which TWO payment types would you recommend for processing using BACS?

	✓
Payment of wages to permanent staff	✓
Top-up of the petty cash	
Payment for fuel for the delivery vans	
Payment to creditors	✓

Task 2.12

The Sale of Goods Act sets out what a customer is entitled to expect when buying goods from a shop.

Which one of the following is NOT one of the conditions set out in the Sale of Goods Act?

	✔
Goods must be of 'satisfactory quality'	
Goods must be of 'fit for purpose'	
Goods must represent 'value for money'	✔
Goods must be 'as described'	

Task 2.13

Dave's Digital often receives payment by cheque in the post.

(a)   List THREE checks the cashier should make when receiving the cheque.

1)   It is in date

2)   It is signed

3)   The words and figures match

(b)   On a cheque what is:

i)   The payee

The person to whom the cheque is payable

ii)   The drawer

The issuer of the cheque

iii)   The drawee

The bank that has to pay the cheque

Task 2.13, continued

(c)   **State THREE other methods of payment customers are likely to use without visiting the shop**

1	Debit Card
2	Credit Card
3	BACS

Task 2.14

David Rouse has agreed to buy a new car for business use. The seller does not want to accept a business cheque and does not want cash.

(a)   **What service is offered by banks would you recommend?**

Bankers Draft

(b)   **What will be the accounting entries required in the Main Ledger to record this purchase? (Ignore VAT)**

Account name	Debit ✓	Credit ✓
Motor Vehicles	✓	
Cash Book		✓

Task 2.15

Name TWO source documents from which a sales invoice might be prepared

1	Purchase Order
2	Quote / Price list / catalogue

Task 2.16

Dave's digitals usually places orders for goods by posting them to its suppliers.

Suggest THREE alternative ways of placing orders for goods

1	Telephone
2	Fax
3	Email/internet

Task 2.17

Purchases Ledger Control

Date 2015	Details	Amount £	Date 2015	Details	Amount £
31 Aug	Purchases returns	679	1 Aug	Balance b/d	111,022
31 Aug	Payments made to creditors	57,279	31 Aug	Credit purchases	67,451
31 Aug	Transfer to sales ledger control	1,100			
31 Aug	Balance c/d	119,415			
		178,473			178,473
			1 Sept	Balance b/d	119,415

(c)   Reconcile the balances shown above with the sales ledger control account balance you have calculated in part (b)

	£
Sales ledger control account balance as at 1 September	119,415
Total of subsidiary sales ledger accounts as at 1 September	119,433
Difference	18

Task 2.17, continued

(d)   Which ONE of the following errors might have caused the difference?

	✓
One of the accounts in the subsidiary ledger has been understated	
One of the accounts in the subsidiary ledger has been overstated	✓
One supplier has offered a discount	
Dave's Digital has underpaid a supplier	
Dave's Digital has overpaid a supplier	

Task 2.18

Date 2015	Details	Bank £	Date 2015	Cheque Number	Details	Bank £
01 Aug	Balance b/f	12,936	3 Aug	237415	Clearvision Ltd	682
21 Aug	Switched On	6,025	3 Aug	237416	P Farnsworth Ltd	542
21 Aug	TVs 4 U	960	7 Aug	237417	Telemagic plc	6,974
22 Aug	Total Entertainment	670	9 Aug	237418	J Baird	377
21 Aug	**Tony's TVs**	**4,500**	17 Aug	237419	C Jenkins	185
21 Aug	**Interest received**	**21**	18 Aug	237420	P Goldmark	230
			21 Aug		**Lincoln Council**	**787**
			21 Aug		**BCM Ltd**	**100**
			21 Aug		**Bank Charges**	**16**
			22 Aug		**Balance c/d**	**15,219**
		25,112				25,112
23 Aug	Balance b/d	15,219				

Task 2.18, continued

(d)   **Prepare a bank reconciliation statement as at 24 July.**

Note:
Do not make any entries in the shaded boxes

Bank reconciliation statement as at 22 August 2015		
Balance per bank statement	£	8,939
Add:		
Name: Switched On	£	6,025
Name: Total Entertainment	£	670
Total to add	£	6,695
Less:		
Name: C Jenkins	£	185
Name: P Goldmark	£	230
Total to subtract	£	415
Balance as per cash book	£	15,219

Task 2.19

DAVE'S DIGITAL

32 Park Street, South Shields, NE33 6TY

Invoice

Number: SV1180
VAT Registration Number 312 6587 41

Invoice to

| Tony's TVs |
| 265 Short Street |
| Dundee |
| DD5 5MY |

Date/ tax point: 1st Sept 2015

Account:

Your reference: 2391

Product Code	Item	Quantity	Price Each	Total
	Scart Leads	6	£ 20.00	£ 120.00
Net Amount				£ 120.00
VAT @ 20%				£ 23.28
Invoice Total				£ 143.28

Terms
   3% settlement discount for settlement within 7 days, other wise 30 days net

(b)   What will be the amount payable if payment is made within 7 days?

£139.68

(c)   What will be the amount payable if payment is NOT made within 7 days?

£143.28

Task 2.20

DAVE'S DIGITAL

32 Park Street,
South Shields,
NE33 6TY

Mr J Baird
Total Entertainment
37 Riverside,
Chester,
CH1 3RD

30th September 2015

Dear Mr Baird,

Further to your recent telephone message, we have pleasure in enclosing our cheque for £50. This represents the balance of your account with us. The account has gone into credit because your last cheque to us was for £990 rather than the £940 owing.

Yours sincerely

Robert Adler
Customer Accounts Manager

Enc: Cheque for £50